Surviving the Death of Your Spouse

A STEP-BY-STEP WORKBOOK

DEBORAH S. LEVINSON, LCSW-C

New Harbinger Publications, Inc.

Publisher's Note

This publication is designed to provide accurate and authoritative information in regard to the subject matter covered. It is sold with the understanding that the publisher is not engaged in rendering psychological, financial, legal, or other professional services. If expert assistance or counseling is needed, the services of a competent professional should be sought.

Cover design by Amy Shoup
Acquired by Melissa Kirk
Edited by Karen O'Donnell Stein
Text design by Tracy Marie Carlson

ISBN 1-57224-377-5 Paperback

Distributed in Canada by Raincoast Books

New Harbinger Publications' Web site address: www.newharbinger.com

06   05   04

10   9   8   7   6   5   4   3   2   1

First printing

This book is dedicated to Elaine Yatzkan and Fern Karesh Hurst, two significant friends who have provided me with the love, structure, and safety net that I needed in order to start a new life in New York. Fern and Elaine, you gave graciously and unobtrusively of yourselves. With your support, I have had the luxury of time and space to be creative. Thank you.

Contents

Part II
Stage 2

Part III
Stage 3

Part IV
The Model in Practice

Foreword

Over the past few decades, research on death and dying issues has dramatically increased in the United States. Hopefully, this may be an indication that our historical reputation as a death-denying culture may be on the wane. We now know more about the sociological and psychological variables associated with adaptation to the loss of significant others. This expanding knowledge has led to the emergence of widespread death education and survivor education programs in the public and private spheres of our society. These have several goals, among which are to assist people in coming to grips with their feelings and attitudes toward death and the dying process, and providing them with the knowledge and skills relevant to adapting to the loss of significant others. *Surviving the Death of Your Spouse: A Step-by-Step Workbook* is one of the latest and most welcome contributions to the growing literature in the area of survivor education. Distinctly pragmatic in orientation, it provides the reader with a precise and easily understood approach to achieving a relatively satisfactory adjustment to the demise of one's spouse.

Based on the author's personal loss of her spouse, as well as her research and clinical practice, this workbook guides the survivor along the path to recovery in a sympathetic and understanding framework of adjustment. Case material from widely diverse real-life situations is utilized throughout to illustrate the major components of that framework. It begins with recognizing the role of a deceased spouse as the anchor—the stabilizing force around which the survivor had previously organized his or her life. When that anchoring quality of a relationship, and its associated attachment, is gone, adjustments must be made if the widowed are to regain some semblance of normalcy in their lives.

Levinson sees the adjustment process generally occurring in three broad stages, each with its own set of skills and tasks, which need to be accomplished before moving to a new stage. In her spousal loss model, changes in the immediate environment initially occur as a result of the spouse's death. When those stabilize, the bereaved then moves on to external personal changes, such as the decision to enter new relationships. In the transition phase of this change journey, the survivor experiences intrapsychic change and achieves a fresh level of emotional growth and development. Then, in the final stage, the person is prepared to integrate their reshaped self and identity with a new environment and way of life. Subsequent chapters describe in clear detail the components of these stages, the tasks associated with each, and a series of exercises that survivors can utilize to develop goals and explore their own lives. A useful set of markers is introduced to define the passage through the adjustment journey, beginning with the trauma, then treading water, the stages of pseudoequilibrium (encompassing the new dating experiences), readying for the transition to liftoff, and finally renewal and resolution.

The book is particularly insightful in anticipating many of the dilemmas and questions that face the surviving spouse. For example, guidelines for establishing, evaluating, renegotiating, and terminating new relationships are specified in extensive discussions of the new social/emotional dating context. Steps are laid out for initiating the important interpersonal change process that eventually leads to a recasting of one's identity. That process, Levinson notes, "is the major task of the transition to liftoff phase of the journey." It is the climax to the story. It parallels the difficult part of a mountain—the summit of the journey. The final phase of the adjustment process, renewal and resolution, is the integration of the different aspects of the change process. The resolution takes place at a new level of emotional growth and development.

Throughout, the survivor is encouraged to engage in the self-evaluation process to deal with the uncertainties of his or her new status of being widowed, and for enhancing emotional and developmental growth. It is recognized that while individuals go through this intrapsychic change journey at their own pace, the experience often appears to be essential to achieving a new and satisfactory balance in the many distinct areas of one's life, especially for women.

The loss of a mate presents the widowed with a range of individual and familial adaptational challenges that require the expenditure of considerable cognitive and emotional effort to resolve. For many, this process of adjustment is often difficult and painful. *Surviving the Death of Your Spouse* offers numerous concrete strategies, tools, and techniques that can be implemented to ease that process and the transitions it encompasses. Those survivors who are attempting to integrate their children into a new family configuration should find these particularly helpful. This volume is particularly informative in its use of numerous stories of the widowed. They clearly demonstrate that the range of adjustments to spousal loss, while exhibiting some commonalities, more often reflects the individual survivor's idiosyncratic circumstances and contingencies—and that is important.

—Felix M. Berardo
    Professor Emeritus, Department of Sociology, University of Florida

Acknowledgments

There are many people who have brought me to the point where I could write this, my second book. First and foremost is Phillip, my friend, lover, and soul mate, who has mentored me and now set me free to do my own thing. There are Maria and Frank, who have encouraged me to pursue my own path and then guided me in the process of crafting a book. There is Eric Schwartz, my intellectual property lawyer, who preserved my creativity for me. There is Tish Wick, who found Eric. And then there is my brother, Lee, who encouraged me to get an intellectual property lawyer, giving me the highest possible compliment from a sibling: "I have never had an original thought to protect. Protect yours."

In addition, there are my many other friends who have encouraged and supported my work. There is Nancy S. Levine, a bright and clever friend who has given of her time to read over my work and provide me with ideas and thoughts and suggestions. There is my longtime friend Jay Farmer, who carefully reviewed my first draft, and Dr. Geoffrey Grief, who patiently continues to find time in his own busy professional schedule to guide me and make suggestions. There is my editor, Melissa Kirk, who has been very gentle in her criticism and suggestions. I am truly touched by her kindness. There is Priscilla Eakley, who unselfishly gave of her professional expertise and advice in this enterprise. There is Evan Wiegand, who tirelessly spent his winter break crafting designs for the exercises.

And then there are my children, Andy, Langley, Jon, and Jennifer, all of whom have supported and encouraged my midlife transitions and changes. (Not everyone's mother leaves home to go start a new life in two new cities without retiring!)

A special thanks to Langley, who cleverly and creatively helped title both books. There are Jinny and Sewell, Rosalie, Betty and Harland, and Uncle Joel—many thanks to them for continuing to offer kindness, support, and words of wisdom as I worked to integrate my new family.

There are countless other friends, such as Ann Saunders, who have supported my research and writing endeavors. In addition, editors at New Harbinger have patiently worked to make this project a reality. To all of you I am grateful. Thank you!

Introduction

I began this journey more than a decade ago, on a beautiful Memorial Day weekend, when my husband of twenty-two years died of cancer, after a one-year illness.

A TERMINAL DIAGNOSIS

Initially, the diagnosis was overwhelming. I could not grasp the enormity of what I was facing. My husband, then age forty-eight, was going to die. I, at age forty-four, was going to be a widow. Our sons, ages fourteen and seventeen, were about to lose their father. Adolescent, vulnerable, searching for an identity, these boys would lose a major advocate, role model, and anchor.

We were supposed to be looking at colleges for my older son, an excellent student with many good schools from which to choose, and helping him in his college selection process. But instead of our focus being on college selection, it was redirected to researching medical-care options and taking my husband to his treatments. The college selection process had to be squeezed in between chemotherapy treatments, infections, doctor visits, and lab tests.

How did I feel? Rarely did I have the time or the luxury to feel at all. I spent most of my time running from one activity to the next. When I stopped running, I felt scared, overwhelmed, and very alone. I was out of sync with my peer group, whom I watched from a distance as they handled normal life-transition issues. I knew that I was in a very different place, dealing with life-and-death matters as my peers helped their children with the college applications or planned vacations.

That year of my husband's illness was a busy time. Each day, all I could do was prioritize my tasks for that day. As the primary caregiver, wife, and mother, I had a full plate of responsibilities. Yet I had a psychotherapy practice to maintain. I knew I would need my practice after my husband died. Also, my practice served as a reality check. I could focus on others' problems instead of my own. It was the only activity I could justify that allowed me to keep in touch with my sense of self. It was my contact with the world of the living. In short, my practice was a useful and necessary diversion. Outside of work, my roles involved caring for others—my husband, my widowed and emotionally dependent mother, and my children. I was the central switchboard and stable base for everyone. I knew I was going to guide my family through unfamiliar territory. I just did what had to be done at the moment and unconsciously deferred processing my feelings until much later.

A Johns Hopkins–trained psychotherapist, I expected to go on with my professional practice in my home town, Baltimore, Maryland. I expected to put my children through college and help them transition to adulthood. I assumed I would adjust to being single. Now, looking back over the years, I realize that I could not have predicted where the journey would take me. I never expected to have the choices I have had or to make the changes I have made.

As a psychotherapist, I have learned about the process involved in making changes in one's life. I have learned about how to focus on the overall process of change and to ignore the day-to-day occurrences that are not important in the larger life scheme. Even with all that knowledge, I was surprised about my own transition and the profound changes that I have experienced.

After my husband died, I continued my practice and later went back to graduate school for my third degree, one in social work, and, more important, for my social work license, my "insurance policy" that would allow me to continue practicing in the changing world of health care. During this transition period, people who had lost their spouses frequently came up to me and asked, "How do I restart my life? You are a widow *and* a psychotherapist, so you must know the answer to the question." These people noted that professionals and books on the subject focused on what to feel, not what to do.

HOW DO YOU RESTART YOUR LIFE?

What a good question, I thought. I continued to think about it over the course of a few years. Later, during my graduate program in social work, I began an independent project, somewhat naively, addressing this project directly. After a few months and several qualitative interviews I became very intrigued. An expanded thesis on this topic became a major motivator in recrafting my professional life.

More specifically, I had to do a paper, a year's work, in order to graduate with my degree in social work. I decided to use the story of one of my patients from my private practice as a focus of the thesis. This patient had been widowed about two years. Traditional theories (Kubler-Ross 1997), suggested that the adjustment to widowhood takes about two years; thus, I assumed that this patient's adjustment should be somewhat on track, yet it was not. On the surface, she was moving along, making some changes, yet emotionally she was not where I had expected her to be. She was struggling. She was sad, lonely, and searching, despite having sold the family home, moved to a new community, and enrolled in vocational school so she could earn a living and support her son. Looking back, I now realize that she was experiencing some change, moving two steps forward and one step back. I learned that adjustment is not contained in a tidy two-year period.

At that point in my personal life, I had developed a relationship with the man who would later become my second spouse. A neuroscientist by training and experienced in basic scientific research, he encouraged me to go out and interview people and see what I could find. I did. I began a series of qualitative interviews as part of a study that would serve as the basis for my first published work and, later, as the foundation of all my research. I interviewed fifteen young widows, all of whom had been widowed more than two years, and found that there was a surprising similarity to the adjustment process they described. From the repetitive pattern that emerged, I was able to formulate a three-stage model that frames the adjustment process after the loss of a spouse. I call this framework the spousal loss model (Levinson 1997). Each interview began with the statement "Tell me your story," and ended with the question "Do you consider your adjustment complete?" I was amazed at the uniformity of the responses. Everyone began with either the sudden onset of the spouse's illness or the spouse's sudden death. I was also struck by the similar threads, themes, and evolving patterns in each story.

The impact that the model had on people was represented a year later at the meetings of the Gerontology Society of America, where I pictorially presented the three stages of the model. I was humbled by the impact of the visual presentation of the model on other professionals—researchers, gerontologists, sociologists, and anthropologists—who reacted in a personal way to the drawings. I watched the faces of those who had been widowed; as they arrived at the depictions of the stage they were currently experiencing themselves, their faces changed dramatically and tears appeared in their eyes. This powerful moment embedded itself in my mind. Those who were not widowed but professionally focused on this life-altering event stopped to talk with me about the impact the visual display had had on them.

My research continued. Departing from the current vogue of using quantitative research (numbers and statistics), I decided to use an older method, namely qualitative research. Thus, I have traveled the country interviewing men and women of all ages to assess the process of their adjustment journey. Most recently, I have begun a study of women who have been widowed more than once in order to assess how they move on with their lives after the death of each spouse and whether the adjustment process differs each time.

In the last few years, I have expanded my talking and lecturing to include multiple cities and venues, both personal and professional. I am enlarging my cache of stories and continue to find that the stories validate the basic themes that will be presented in this book.

What I have learned through my personal and professional journey is that grief and mourning are just a part of the process of change. One psychotherapist is quoted as saying that all of therapy is about adjusting to loss (Paul and Paul 1975). The adjustment process, as I envision it, is forward moving, allowing the widowed person to look for light, hope, and beauty at the end of a dark period in his or her life. This book does not focus on loss and its emotions; it considers emotions in the context of concrete tasks and skills that need to be accomplished in the transition process. This book is upbeat and it focuses on the light and hope you experience as you emerge from a tunnel of darkness. A participant at a recent presentation regarding my three-stage model of adjusting to loss put it succinctly: "You give vision and hope to an otherwise dreary future."

AN EPIDEMIOLOGICAL VIEW

As a result of the terrorist attacks of September 11, 2001, in the United States, the world has changed dramatically. We are now living in a world where change is constant; the unexpected, a given. The events of September 11, 2001, caused temporary chaos as Americans adjusted to the fact that security and safety on American shores were no longer a given. Before 9/11, a young person experiencing the loss of a spouse was a rarity. After 9/11, loss of a spouse at a young age became a national problem, part of a group consciousness.

And with the advent of the Iraq war in 2003, loss of American soldiers' lives have made young widow- and widowerhood an even larger part of the national consciousness.

A more generic focus on widows and widowers in our society is fostered by the increasing numbers of people living productive lives into their nineties.

OLDER WIDOWS AND WIDOWERS

The number of American people, especially women, who have lost a spouse is increasing. In the 1990 census 1 million women of all ages listed themselves as widows (Rosenberg 1991). In the 2000 census more than 11 million women identified themselves as widows. The census data also indicates that more than 2 million men are widowed (U.S. Census Bureau 2000).

Initial research on widowhood in the 1970s described a woman's experience after the death of her spouse as generally an accommodation to her new single life; remarriage was not the norm (Lopata 1973, 1996). Today, women widowed in their fifties and sixties are still young. Epidemiological studies predict that more and more people will be living good, productive lives well into their nineties and that more people in their seventies and eighties are looking for companion. Thus, widowed people in their fifties and sixties may still have twenty to forty more years to devote to new relationships and pursuits. As people age, how can they continued to lead productive lives and form constructive relationships in their later years? The model presented in this book is a useful framework for people to use to create a new chapter in their life, irrespective of age.

THE PURPOSE OF THE BOOK

This book is meant to give you an opportunity to create a new chapter in your life following the death of your spouse. This book offers a basic framework that you may use to craft your own personal change journey, unique to your needs, desires, and expectations. So if you focus on the journey, your new life will unfold in time.

How to Use the Book

This workbook serves as a guidebook. Just as you might use a travel book to guide you through a foreign city, use this book to guide your travels as you make this life transition. It gives structure to your journey, yet allows you the freedom to make the journey uniquely yours. Put the book in a familiar, accessible place in your home. Remember to refer back to it as needed, rereading those sections that apply to your particular point in the journey.

Each stage of the adjustment process comes with a series of skills and tasks that need to be completed in order for you to move to the next stage of the journey. The first stage after your spouse dies, called *treading water*, involves simply putting one foot in front of the other. The second stage, called *pseudoequilibrium,* is the time when you begin to experience personal change. Women who choose to date may experience emotional growth during the *transition to liftoff* period (an interim phase between the second and third stages) and emerge from the process at a new level of emotional development. At that point, a woman will be ready to experience the third and final stage of the process, *renewal and resolution.* Although most men do not need to experience the transition to liftoff phase of the process, after the pseudoequilibrium stage they too will be ready to enter the renewal and resolution stage. This book will explore each stage and its tasks and offer stories illustrating both what to do and what not to do in order to build your new life. The journey will become uniquely your own as you apply your lifestyle issues and individual story to each step of the process.

Who Should Read This Book

This book is written primarily for men and women whose spouse has died. However, people who have experienced divorce or the ending of a long-term relationship may also find it helpful. Although my work has primarily been with heterosexual couples, the principles of the model may also be applied to same-sex relationships.

People who have lost a child may also be helped by the ideas in this book. Below are some examples of people who may benefit from using this model.

One young divorcée told me that her divorce was like a death—she never saw or had contact with her ex-spouse again. A widow whose husband died five years ago confided that now that her youngest child is in his last year of high school, she feels ready to focus on herself, something that has not been easy for her to do. A widower who had read my first book, *The Next Beginning* (2002), noted that the discussion of the emotions experienced by young widows could apply to him too. No matter whom you have lost, you'll benefit from reading this book.

When to Read This Book

The book seems most useful beginning two months after a spouse's death. Before then, you will probably have difficulty concentrating and absorbing what you read, and the information in the book may be too painful while the trauma of loss is so new and fresh. After a couple of months, you'll be more ready to begin the adjustment process and use the information in this book.

One bit of advice: the transition journey you are about to begin is hard work. The exercises in this book may appear easy, but they are designed to get you to both think and feel. To get the best results, take time to think about each question thoroughly before answering it.

You may read the book any of several ways. You may quickly read through the whole book once and then go back and read one chapter at a time, taking a moment to do the exercises. Or you may jump ahead to the end while you are still in the middle. Finally, you may choose to take one chapter at a time, leaving the end for last. It's your choice. Choose the reading style that works for you.

So now, put your travel hat on, begin reading, and begin your journey. Good luck!

Part I

Stage 1

Chapter 1

Two Themes: The Anchor and the Journey

THE ANCHOR

Your spouse was an anchor, the person around whom you organized your world. The connection started as a conscious attachment, but the depth and quality of the connection developed over time and eventually became a part of your unconscious. In fact, you may have even taken it for granted. Now you are faced with living your life without your partner.

Recall your life six months before your spouse died. There was a certain order or routine to how your life worked. There may have been occasional changes and variations to the routine, but you could count on a certain stability, predictability, and structure in your life together. Now, stop a moment and answer the questions below to help you examine how your daily life has changed since your spouse died.

Your Daily Routine before Your Spouse Died

1. What time did you get up in the morning? _____

2. Did you have coffee or breakfast with your spouse? _____

3. Did your spouse go to work? _____

4. What time did he or she leave for work? _____

5. Did you go to work? If so, what time did you leave? _____

6. If you did not work, what activities did you do during the day (for example, work out at the gym, have lunch with friends, volunteer at the church)? ____
   _____

7. Did you and your spouse see each other in the evening? _____

8. Did you have dinner together? _____

9. Who cooked? _____

10. What time did you eat together? _____

11. Did you watch TV together? _____

12. Did you sleep together in the same bed? _____

13. Did you spend weekends and holidays together? _____

14. Did you spend summers together? _____

15. Did you vacation together? How? _____

16. Did you have favorite vacation spots that you visited at special times? _____
    _____

Likely, all of these activities helped define the structure of your day, your week, your month, and your year. After your spouse died, the structure of your life changed.

Now pick a period of time, perhaps three months, after your spouse died. Answer the following questions regarding that period of time.

1. What time do you get up in the morning? _____

2. Do you go out for coffee or breakfast? _____

3. How do you spend your day? At work? Doing volunteer activities? Exercising?
   _____

4. Do you see friends during these activities? _____

5. What do you do for dinner in the evening? Do you eat alone? At home? Do you cook? _____

6. What do you do after dinner? Watch TV? If so, do you watch alone? Do you watch the same shows you watched or do the same evening activities you did while your spouse was alive? _____

7. How do you end your evening (for example, call your adult children, read, go to sleep in a different bed from the one you slept in when your spouse was alive)? _____

8. How do you spend your time on weekends? _____

9. On holidays? _____

10. What do you do for vacations? _____

11. How do these vacation activities differ from what you did while your spouse was alive? _____

Compare your answers to the first and second set of questions. How many of these daily activities are different from those you engaged in when your husband was alive?

The purpose of this exercise is for you to be able to get a basic concrete picture of your daily life both before and after the death of your spouse. Mark this page; you'll return to it later on in the book. Now, let's look at the many ways, obvious and subtle, in which you were dependent on your spouse.

Your spouse, the stabilizing force around whom you organized your life, is gone. Regardless of the quality of the relationship—good, bad, happy, or conflictual—the loss of your spouse, your anchor, throws your life into chaos (Butz 1992).

I remember Maddie's story. She called and told me that her husband, who had been diagnosed with colon cancer six months before, had died. During his illness Maddie had handled herself well. She was strong and solid, and she stood by his side. She was sad, but she felt confident with regard to her ability to adapt and adjust to his death. When he was in the hospital for the last time, she got in bed with him and gently told him he could die, that she would be okay.

For two weeks after he died, Maddie was fine. Then, suddenly confused and disoriented, she fell apart. Thought she did not realize it, her anchor was gone. Her reaction surprised her, since she had not been consciously aware of being dependent on him to get through her day. She had gone about her daily business by herself, doing housework, running her home day care, going grocery shopping, and paying the bills. Her husband had gone to work every day, would come home in the evening, and would eat dinner with her. But although Maddie had appeared to function independently, she was emotionally dependent on her spouse. Once he was dead, she was no longer able to function as she had before. She was anxious and surprised at her own behavior. Now Maddie had to learn how to cope with her world without her husband as an anchor.

Maddie's story shows how your spouse serves as a stable base. Other stories in the book will illustrate that the quality of the relationship (good or bad) is separate from the anchoring role your spouse played.

ATTACHMENT

Why is your life in chaos after your spouse dies? Because your spouse was an attachment object, the significant person to whom you are connected, probably on a deep and largely unconscious level.

You may more easily understand this idea if you think about the connection between a young child and his or her primary caregiver or parent. According to some theorists, this attachment takes place during the bonding process between ages four and seven months, as part of the infant's emotional development. Later in life, the child transfers this attachment to other significant people in his or her life. A first boyfriend or girlfriend may become a transitional attachment object in adolescence. This attachment is frequently the connection that allows an adolescent to begin to separate from his or her parents. Later, other attachments become primary—a significant other in early adulthood, and, subsequently, a spouse.

Attachments over Your Life Span

List your attachments over your lifetime below.

Developmental Stage of Life	Your Attachment	Example
Infancy	_____	Parent or caregiver
Early childhood	_____	Parent or caregiver
Teenage years	_____	Boyfriend, girlfriend, pet, or best friend
Early adulthood	_____	Significant boyfriend or girlfriend
Middle adulthood	_____	Spouse, pet, child, parent
Late adulthood	_____	Adult child, spouse, companion, or pet

The concept of an attachment object was written about by John Bowlby (1969, 1973, 1980) who studied children who were evacuated from London in World War II during the blitzkreig. Bowlby studied the detachment and resulting depression that appeared in children who were separated from their parents during this period. His work forms the basis of many theories about attachment, loss, and subsequent adjustment.

Bowlby noticed that when separated from their parents, children initially became withdrawn and detached from their environment. Later, they became depressed, being described as sad and disorganized. Some time thereafter, the children recovered from their depression, regrouped, and were reintegrated into their world. In my interviews with men and women who had lost their spouse at least two years beforehand, I found that their descriptions of their experiences closely resembled Bowlby's description of the loss and adjustment process of children who had been separated from their parents.

Take a few moments and review your life. In a notebook, write down losses you may have experienced at different times in your life. For example, suppose a childhood friend moved away. Or another friend may have died from leukemia. Perhaps as a teenager, you lost a close classmate in a car accident. Perhaps as an adult you have experienced the loss of a parent. In the exercise below, compare the feelings you remember experiencing around each loss. Now think about the death of your spouse. Compare how you felt about your spouse's death with your feelings around other losses you have experienced.

Early Losses

Loss: _____

Describe feelings you remember having around this loss: _____

_____

_____

Loss: _____

Describe feelings you remember having around this loss: _____

_____

_____

Loss: _____

Describe feelings you remember having around this loss: _____

_____

_____

Loss of Spouse: _____

Describe feelings you remember having around the loss of your spouse: _____

_____

_____

The purpose of this exercise is to help you see how your feelings may differ from one loss to another, and especially how your feelings about the loss of your spouse contrast with the feelings about other losses. Losses come in categories, with differences in degree and kind. While you may have been very close to a friend who died when you were a child, that loss is probably very different in kind from the loss of a parent or spouse. Highlighting the differences in losses is another way to understand the depth and breadth of the loss of your spouse, your anchor.

WHEN THE MARRIAGE WAS DIFFICULT

Even if your marriage was not ideal, you likely relied upon your spouse as an anchor, and the loss of that anchor is no less devastating than it would be for someone with a good marriage.

The stories below may illustrate the anchoring quality of a spouse even in the face of possible divorce.

Charlie and Joyce were a married couple in their late thirties. Charlie had recently transitioned from a lucrative career as a physician to a lower-paying career as a religious teacher. Despite the fact that his new job was located in another city (requiring him to spend the workweek away from home) and did not pay enough to support his family, he was determined to leave medicine. Joyce agreed to Charlie's career change on a trial basis.

For Joyce, the stress of managing the household, caring for the children, juggling expenses on a very limited income, and taking care of her own work, all without her husband's help, was enormous. Making things worse was Charlie's tendency to criticize Joyce and undermine her parenting. Joyce was able to stand Charlie's critical behavior, though, until the death of her father, an important figure in her life.

Joyce and Charlie came to me for help with their relationship. Several weeks afterward Joyce called to say that Charlie was critically ill. He died one week later. Joyce was shocked and devastated by Charlie's untimely death. Now a widow, Joyce had to figure out how to make a life for herself and her large family on limited financial resources. During this period Joyce came back to therapy with me to deal with her loss and to make some plans for her future.

Even though Charlie's behavior toward Joyce had left a lot to be desired, during my therapy sessions with Joyce she recalled the close friendship she and Charlie had had, including their ritual of going to a neighborhood ice cream parlor and sharing a pint of ice cream while they talked about their day. That piece of their relationship she would dearly miss.

Joyce's story shows that when we're angry we don't always recall the good aspects of our spouse and our relationship. It is only after the relationship ends that memories of these special times in the relationship reemerge. Charlie was Joyce's anchor and her friend, and she missed him greatly.

Another interesting story was Laura's. Laura's husband was significantly older than her and she acknowledged to me that she had married him because she had been looking for a father figure. First, Laura, and then her husband, came in to therapy to talk about his habit of controlling both Laura and their son. After a few sessions, Laura's husband tried to tone down his controlling behavior, and they stopped coming to therapy.

Several years later I heard from Laura again. Her husband had been treated for cancer, which was now in remission. She hoped it would stay that way. A year or so later, Laura called me again, very upset, to say that her husband was dying, and she would be left alone to raise her son.

After her husband died, Laura came in to see me. She told me that she and her husband had resolved their differences as he was dying. He had left her sufficient resources to go back to school and develop a career so that she could support herself and her son. She was planning to find a new place to live in a suitable neighborhood because she wanted her son to grow up in a good environment. She told me that she would eventually look for another relationship, but for the time being she would focus on herself and her son.

Despite her apparent sanguine attitude, Laura was sad about her husband's death. Although her husband had been controlling and had made her angry, he was a stable base. She could always count on him. She had not realized how much she depended on him as an anchor. Now he was gone. It was quite overwhelming for her to deal with the fact that he was gone forever.

These stories illustrate that even a spouse in a troubled marriage can provide a stable base, and when that base is taken away the world of the surviving spouse is thrown into chaos.

A THREE-STAGE JOURNEY

It is obvious to most that after a spouse dies, your life changes (Alan 1994; Kohak 1994). The question is what happens and whether you can affect the process. The short answer is that yes, you can affect what happens. The long answer is that there appears to be a three-stage pattern to the process of change. The movement from one stage to the next, however, does not need to be linear, or time specific. A person may be in one stage, move to the second, then go back to the first stage, and later move forward to the third. Now, let us take a look at each stage in turn.

Treading Water

The first step in the adjustment process begins immediately with the death of your spouse. The first stage is rather like treading water (Levinson 1997). All you can do is keep your head above water until the environment restabilizes. After the death of your spouse your world is in chaos and makes little sense to you. You may feel disorganized, disoriented, and unable to concentrate, with no structure or direction. You may even be unsure about the meaning of your life. The chaos feels uncomfortable. Some people report that this feeling of chaos makes them feel crazy, and many say they simply feel confused. You may find yourself asking, What am I supposed to do? Where am I supposed to go?

During this treading water stage, which may take quite some time, concentrate on simply putting one foot in front of the other, taking one day, or even one minute, at a time, until a new structure emerges. Your tasks during the treading water stage include taking care of business matters, such as arranging for the funeral, concluding your spouse's business matters, and dealing with his or her estate.

You may be wondering how long you will spend in this stage. The amount of time spent treading water varies from person to person—it may take two weeks to several years. For example, a person whose spouse had Alzheimer's disease for five years may find that the spouse's death is a "nonevent"; two weeks after the funeral the surviving spouse may actually have a new routine in place and be ready to enter stage two of the adjustment process, where he or she will make personal changes. However, if a spouse dies suddenly at age thirty-six, the surviving spouse may be numb and in shock for a year or more before a new routine emerges and allows him or her to enter stage two and address personal change.

In this stage you begin mourning your spouse, a process that is more complex than just the initial grief. Mourning itself is only one aspect of the adjustment process. While there may be sadness, tears, sorrow, and grief in the weeks, months, or years after the spouse dies, at the funeral and immediately afterward a surviving spouse may be too numb to express sadness—instead she or he may feel nothing or only anxiety. As you will see, grief and mourning take place at different times and change character during each stage of adjustment (Horowitz 1990; Marwit and Klass 1995).

Pseudoequilibrium

In the second stage, pseudoequilibrium, which takes place after a new, albeit temporary, sense of order has been established in your life, you will begin to address personal change as an individual without your spouse. During this period you will probably try on new "faces" to see what fits. We call this period *pseudo*equilibrium, however, because your new and transitional sense of stability may turn out to be elusive. New faces you try initially you may discard later in your adjustment journey. While you may feel as though your life is coming together, you still have a ways to go.

This stage has two parts. The tasks of the initial phase of the pseudoequilibrium stage have to do with external personal change and may include sampling new activities, new adventures, and new aspects of your identity. For example, you may redecorate a room in your house, or you may learn to fix a flat tire. You may decide to take a day trip to a nearby city to see a play, or go to a movie alone.

Transition to Liftoff

During the second phase of the pseudoequilibrium stage you may tackle bigger adventures, like traveling to an exotic place, or taking up an activity that you might never have considered in your marriage. At some point in this second phase of stage two you might decide to date and even enter a relationship. Frequently the relationship, formed at a vulnerable time, will run its course and end, especially for women. The ending of the relationship will catapult you into a dynamic emotional growth process, the next part of the transition process.

The climax of the journey is the transition to liftoff stage. The ending of your first significant relationship after the death of your spouse initiates this dynamic internal personal change process, from which you will grow and emerge at a new level of emotional development. You will then feel ready to meet and greet the world again. At that time you may connect with a new person, with whom you will form a more meaningful relationship. At that point you will enter the third and final stage of your journey, renewal and resolution.

Renewal and Resolution

During the third stage you will integrate your children into your new life. You will relegate your memories of your spouse to your history. You will have a new anchor and a new structure or meaning to your life. Your life and your patterns of daily living will have a new flavor and quality to them that have nothing to do with your late spouse.

I remember asking Polly, who never dated or took on new adventures after her husband, Frank, died, how she made a particular decision. She answered that she had tried to imagine what Frank would recommend if he were alive. She continued to use Frank as a frame of reference even forty years after his death. In contrast, Wanda, who tried out new relationships, skills, and activities after she lost her husband, told me that her new life has no resemblance to her former life. She even lives in another city. Integrating a changed self with a changed world is a unique challenge.

The three-stage spousal loss model is a framework for the change journey you may take, although the exact nature of your personal journey within this framework will be your own. The change process should be tackled one step at a time. It is important to realize the enormity of the task. Do not try to do too much at any one time. Rather, establish a series of small goals so that you can see some progress and feel a sense of accomplishment as you go along on your life change journey.

Now that I have given you an overview of your adjustment journey, I will take each stage of the journey and describe it in detail in the chapters that follow. I will outline the tasks of each stage so that you can develop your own goals. I will offer exercises that will help you examine your thoughts and feelings over the course of your journey; you'll explore the things you have done, skills you have gained, and pleasures you have discovered, so that you may use these discoveries as you craft your new life.

Chapter 2

Stage One: Treading Water

Your journey begins with your spouse's death. Numb and in shock, you may feel as if you're operating on automatic pilot. You make funeral and burial arrangements, receive condolences, and talk to visitors, not quite knowing exactly how you feel. Once the funeral is over and family and friends have gone home, however, you begin to face living life alone without your spouse.

THE FUNERAL

If you are a member of an organized religion, you may follow the funeral or burial rituals prescribed by your religious affiliation. Rituals at this time are useful and purposeful, providing structure during a time of change. For example, many religions have coming-of-age rituals and ceremonies marking the change of seasons. Similarly, the funeral ritual marks the end of your spouse's life and the beginning of your transition and adjustment. The funeral ritual provides focus, structure, and a framework for activity after major loss, which helps to decrease your anxiety. In preparing for the funeral, you and your family members have to focus on concrete immediate decisions, such as how to eulogize the deceased, what prayers are to be recited, what poems are to be read, and who will speak.

Creating a eulogy is a beneficial task that helps you and other mourners review and highlight what was important about the deceased person's life. It is a way of processing who your spouse was. The review process helps focus the dialogue and you may find that it brings family members together, at least for the moment. Tears that are shed during this process serve as a release of the emotional tension that builds up as you deal with the reality that your anchor has died.

When you're working on the eulogy, you may want to consider concentrating on the topics listed below—they may help you figure out how to sum up your spouse's life. Another way of organizing your thoughts for the eulogy is to write an essay about your spouse utilizing the topics below. This exercise is also a good method of processing your loss. You do not have to do this essay all in one sitting, nor do you have to share it with others unless you choose to. It can be as short or as long as you wish.

Topics to Be Considered for Inclusion in a Eulogy

Childhood

Family of origin

Young adulthood

Work

Family and relationships

What was important to the deceased

How you were touched by the deceased

How you will remember the deceased

Stories that help characterize the deceased's life

Eulogy or Essay

What you wish to say:

_____

_____

_____

_____

_____

_____

_____

Use extra paper if necessary.

A traditional burial ritual is one way of handling a funeral ritual; cremation and memorial services are another. The purpose of ritual surrounding the death is to give you an immediate focus. As time passes, you may acquire more distance from the trauma and be able to begin to process your loss.

You may find that meeting and greeting people who come to visit and acknowledge your spouse's death takes your attention, energy, and time. It creates a useful diversion, albeit temporary, from the new vacuum in your life. Those first few days, you'll probably have a houseful of visitors. Keeping them fed is also a concrete diversion, which contrasts with your unknown future without your spouse. These kinds of distractions are often actually beneficial, since at this point you may not be ready to fully comprehend the overwhelming change that's happened in your life.

Grace's experience is an example of how the pressing details of the funeral can provide focus and distraction during this bewildering, chaotic time. When her young husband passed away suddenly, after an illness of only three weeks, Grace was devastated. Her Jewish religious practices dictated that the funeral and official mourning period be her immediate focus. Her thoughts on what she would do and how she would manage over the long haul as a widow were put on hold. Hundreds of people came to visit, and Grace was truly distracted. It was not until after the mourning period that she had the time to face the really major practical issues—how would she make it financially, physically, and emotionally on her own?

MOURNING

When a person close to you dies, you may experience immediate grief, or you may feel numb, anxious, or in shock.

Mourning is a process that takes place over a long period of time, according to many theorists. Why? For a person whose spouse has died, mourning involves the loss of both a close loved one and of an anchor—the major stabilizing force around whom the person has organized his or her daily life.

Different theorists interpret the mourning process in different ways. Elisabeth Kubler-Ross (1997) says that when mourning a loss people experience five stages of emotion: denial, sadness, anger, bargaining, and finally acceptance. Kubler-Ross notes that the progression through the stages does not have to be consecutive. One may experience first one stage and then the next, then go back to the first, and finally skip to the fourth and fifth stages. There is no one orderly or uniform process you will experience.

Mardi Horowitz (1990), another theorist, notes that as a person gets further and further from the loss of a loved one, he or she views the person from different perspectives at various stages along the way. This allows the person to conceptualize the loss differently with each new perspective. Thus with more distance from the loss, an individual can visit the lost loved one from an intellectual or cognitive perspective and not just from an emotional perspective (Marwit and Klass 1995).

This idea is more closely related to theories about post-traumatic stress disorder. Certainly, the loss of a close loved one is comparable to any major trauma. At first one is numb and in shock. The trauma to the ego is enormous, so the person builds walls to protect the ego and just puts one foot in front of the other until he or she can get some distance from the traumatic event. At that point, the individual may experience some sadness, pain, or grief. With more distance between him or her and the event, an individual can begin to more effectively process the trauma by looking at it intellectually just like you view a movie on a screen. In this way, the ego is more protected and can cope with the loss more effectively. Then the person is able to process the loss and experience the feelings associated with the loss.

Although grief and mourning are a normal way of dealing with loss, the process may be very painful. The symptoms you may experience when you mourn the loss of a loved one frequently mirror those experienced by people suffering from depression (DSM-IV 1994), and their treatment may also be similar. For this reason, you may benefit from medicine or psychotherapy just as people experiencing a major depression may benefit from treatment.

So how do you feel when you are depressed? Sad, or angry, or perhaps both. You may not be able to concentrate on anything significant, or even read a book or follow a movie. You may not feel like doing anything or being around other people. So what do you do? You just put one foot in front of the other and take one step at a time. Allow some time to pass, and eventually you'll be ready to examine and process your feelings. Remember that there are no right or wrong feelings—feelings are irrational. But it is important to distinguish how you feel from how you act based on your feelings. Let's take a look at the emotions that may come up around your spouse's death.

Feelings

It's often helpful to be aware of your feelings and behavior during stressful times, since it may help you to figure out how to cope. Understanding your feelings also helps you to recognize that what you are experiencing is normal for a person in your situation.

The next section identifies and describes different feelings people may experience when in mourning.

Sadness

It is very normal to feel sad after the loss of a spouse. People experience and express sadness differently. Some people may cry, either a great deal or just a little. Others simply feel a terrible dull ache in their chest or stomach area; this ache is what may be referred to as psychic pain—the pain of loss. Still others feel very tired and lethargic.

After her husband died, Darlene felt intense sadness right away. She wept at the funeral and as she watched the coffin being lowered into the ground. But after the funeral she found that her sadness became less intense, and she would have a crying spell only every few days. After a month, her crying ceased, and she would only cry when she encountered a specific reminder of something about her husband.

Carolyn was different. She found herself shedding only a few tears at the funeral, but she felt very anxious and could not sit or stand still. When she felt sad, the feeling would come up suddenly and then quickly recede. When she visited a garden planted in her husband's memory, for example, she was suddenly overcome by sadness and broke down, but she soon recovered. As the months passed, her fits of intense sadness and tearful moments lessened and gradually dissipated, but her anxiety continued.

As you can see, sadness manifests itself in different ways in each person. If you find, however, that several months after your spouse dies you are still crying every day, you may want to check with your physician to see if he or she would recommend medicine, psychotherapy, or both.

Anger

Many people who have lost a spouse feel anger over being abandoned, even thought they know it is an irrational feeling. They may also feel guilty for being angry since they know that their spouse did not intend to die (except in the case of suicide) and thus abandon them. However, they cannot help feeling angry and thus are conflicted by their mixed feelings. It's important to remember that all of your feelings are valid.

But how can you express your anger appropriately in this situation? To express your anger in an acceptable way, you may find it helpful to understand the two basic components of anger: physical tension, and the angry feelings themselves. The length of time your anger lasts depends on how deep an ego insult your anger represents. Getting rid of the physical tension that builds up when you are angry, either through exercise or an action such as pounding a pillow, may help you feel calmer. In a calmer state, you are better prepared to express your feelings, either verbally or in writing. Although we cannot control how we feel, we can control how we act on our feelings. Try to find safe, acceptable ways to release tension when you're angry so that you can feel free to express your feelings without hurting yourself or others.

Anxiety

Mourning the death of a close loved one, particularly a spouse, means mourning the loss of an attachment object, an anchor. This naturally brings up feelings of anxiety. The anxiety may be quite pervasive and stay with you at all times, or it may come and go in waves. It may only appear at certain times in the day, such as when your spouse would normally have arrived home from work.

The anxiety may even arise in the middle of the night. During sleep, your unconscious mind is free and you are not exerting control over what you are thinking and feeling. Thus, you may not be conscious of anxious feelings suppressed during your busy day that may surface and even cause you to wake up. The early morning hours are usually the time when grieving spouses feel the most anxiety.

Because sufficient sleep is important in your healing process, if you keep waking up in the wee hours of the morning, you may want to consult with your doctor. Both excessive sleep and pervasive anxiety may be signs of depression. A doctor can help you distinguish whether your sleep or anxiety is normal and healthy and may suggest medicine or other methods for you to get a good night's sleep.

Denial

Denial is a coping mechanism that almost everyone uses at some time, particularly when dealing with a traumatic event. It allows a person to postpone looking at reality until he or she is better able to deal with it. Joseph's story is an example of denial.

Joseph was playing golf when he received a call notifying him that his father had been rushed to the hospital. But instead of leaving the golf course immediately to join his father at the hospital, Joseph continued playing golf. He talked about his putt, his drive, the score, the national news, and the local election, but he did not mention his father's name at all. As long as he did not think about it, he did not have to face his father's illness.

Fear

Fear, a protective device, is a feeling that may be triggered when we are thrust into a new and unfamiliar experience. Experiencing a major life change such as the death of your spouse may make you fearful about the changes you face as you begin life alone after many years with a partner. You may be able to get over your fear by learning to do new things and taking risks. See chapter 3 for more discussion of risk taking.

Guilt

Guilt comes from the belief that you should have done something different or made another choice. Guilty feelings result from inner tapes you have incorporated beginning in early childhood that govern your actions.

After your spouse dies, it's quite natural for you to wonder what you might have done that would have prevented your spouse's death. You may think, "If only I had insisted that he go to the internist," or "If only I had made her see the gynecologist, she might still be alive," or "If only it were me and not him." You may also feel guilty for how you treated or felt toward your loved one while he or she was alive.

Elizabeth was the sole caregiver for her mother, who had been critically ill for a long time. Elizabeth was exhausted from being in charge of her mother's care around the clock for so long. Brought up in a family where emotions were not expressed, she believed that she should suppress her feelings and just take care of her mother without complaining. Despite this belief, and despite her knowledge that her mother couldn't help being ill, she couldn't help feeling angry—which led her to also feel guilty.

So, what do you do with your guilt feelings?

First, you need to determine where the guilt is coming from. Does it emanate from an old tape from childhood? If so, ask yourself whether its message really applies to you now. If the guilt results from the current situation, remember this: You always have two choices—you can beat yourself up over something you cannot change, or you can say, "I did the best I could at the moment. Hindsight is always wonderful, but I have to move forward. All I can do is make today the first day of my new life. And each day hereafter is part of my new beginning."

Feelings Barometer

The purpose of the feelings barometer is to quantify how you feel at a given point in time. You may assess your feelings as you travel your journey at different points in time. Take a moment. Assess your intensity of each feeling and mark the date in the appropriate box. At different points in your journey, return to this exercise. At any time, you may compare the difference in the intensity of your feelings.

Now that you have charted your feelings and noted the level of intensity, consider doing something to help you deal with your feelings. You may want to do some vigorous exercise, write down what you feel, talk to a friend, join a support group, or seek psychotherapy or ask your physician about medicine for anxiety, depression, or lack of sleep. Taking action in this way can help you feel less overwhelmed by your feelings as you continue to adjust to the death of your spouse.

How People Mourn Differently

In some cases where the illness is drawn out over a long time, mourning actually begins before the death. I know a woman whose spouse had Alzheimer's disease and lingered for fifteen years. For her, she said, her husband died many times. Each time he lost a part of himself, she mourned. At one stage he lost his physical independence, and she mourned. At another stage he lost his ability to think and make decisions; she mourned. At still another stage he did not remember her anymore; again she mourned. When he finally died, his death was more of a relief to her. She actually said that his death was a nonevent.

On the other hand, when there is sudden death or a brief illness, mourning usually begins with the spouse's death. The suddenness of the event adds to the trauma. There is no time to prepare or say good-bye.

In some cases, people delay mourning. Cathy's father died when she was little. There was no funeral or memorial service. His body was removed from the house and he just disappeared. Cathy's mother never acknowledged her husband's death, saying instead that her husband was away in Ohio.

Recently another woman told me her story. She reported that after her mother's death when she was eight years old, her father told her that her mother had gone away. Confused, the girl spent the next four years looking for her mother and waiting for her return. She was confused because she knew that her mother would never voluntarily

Feelings Chart

Intensity	Sadness	Anger	Fear	Denial	Guilt	Anxiety
10						
9						
8						
7						
6						
5						
4						
3						
2						
1						

Most

Least

Place a date in the box

leave her, so she kept searching. Eventually, at age twelve, she realized that her mother had died, and she finally mourned and tried to move on with her life. But even today, in her fifties, the woman notes that occasionally she will find herself unconsciously looking through a crowd as though she is searching for her mother.

In both of these examples, the surviving spouses did not allow themselves to talk about their loss. Talking about your feelings and about death is a healthy way to approach the issue. It gives you and your loved ones permission to mourn, each in your own way. In my experience as a therapist, talking about difficult issues like death usually results in people feeling better. It does not make the matter go away, but the conversation provides a vehicle for expressing feelings. When people avoid talking about feelings, they get stuck emotionally and are unable to move on with their lives.

People who have experienced the death of a loved one early in life seem to mature as a result of the experience. They learn that death is a part of life, and learning to cope with death in a healthy way helps them live life more richly and adapt to significant life changes effectively.

Identify Your Feelings

What feelings have you experienced when dealing with your spouse's death? Identify them below:

1. _____

2. _____

3. _____

4. _____

5. _____

A reminder: You may be unaware of your feelings early in the transition period because you are numb and in shock. As you become aware of those feelings, come back to this exercise and jot them down. Some people talk about their feelings with others, other people journal their feelings, and still others are just aware of them. Whichever mode suits you, use it. The purpose of this exercise is to make you aware of your feelings as you continue to do the tasks that are a part of this transition journey.

AFTER THE PEOPLE LEAVE

After the funeral and any other mourning rituals, the friends and relatives who have gathered around you go home. You are left alone. Your voice echoes in the silence. Thus, the adjustment process begins. You are immediately confronted with concrete reminders that your spouse is gone. No one to drink coffee with in the morning. No one to come home to in the evening. Going to bed alone knowing your spouse will never walk through the door again. In concrete ways you experience what *forever* means.

Getting through the day at this stage may not be easy. Two things are important to do. The first is that you sleep at night; if you are not sleeping you may want to ask your medical doctor for some appropriate medicine. The second is that you eat during the day. You may still be numb and in shock and so you may not feel hungry. But it is important that you continue to eat and drink during the period following the funeral.

Beginning your life again after the funeral is difficult. The way to do it is make only short-term goals for yourself until you are in a better place for making long-range decisions.

Alice's youngest son was entering his senior year of high school, applying to college, and getting ready to leave home. Alice, having just completed her graduate program, was about to do her social work internship so she could work after her son went off to college. Then Alice's husband was diagnosed with cancer. Alice put her internship on hold while she confronted her husband's illness. Alice just put one foot in front of the other and took one day at a time. Her husband died four months after being diagnosed.

Major loss and major change became the order of the day. Alice's husband, her anchor, had died. Her youngest son finished high school, graduated, and left for college. Her role as a wife had ended and her role as a mother had changed dramatically, leaving her to experience the empty-nest syndrome as a recent widow. Then, one and a half years later, her mother died. Alice had had three major losses within a very short period of time.

Alice continued to put one foot in front of the other, dealing with one major transition at a time. Each loss placed her in a position of having to establish a new routine before she could attend to personal change.

Evette's story is slightly different. Evette and her husband were at a baseball game when he suddenly collapsed and died. She had no time to say good-bye or prepare for her husband's death. One day her husband was there, and the next day he was gone. It took all of her energy just to get through the day after her husband died.

Josh described a different situation. After caring for his wife at home for some time, he finally reached the point where he could no longer shoulder the burden alone. It was then that he placed her in an Alzheimer's facility. She no longer recognizes him when he visits, and so he has essentially said his good-byes to her. Although no burial ritual can be held to help bring him closure, Josh must start his life again in some form while his wife is still alive. As you can see, the nature of the illness and how your spouse dies may define part of your adjustment process.

Taking Care of Business

As soon as the funeral ritual is over, you'll find yourself faced with many business and financial decisions and tasks. Unfortunately (or maybe fortunately), attending to business is a primary task of this treading water stage. While you may have a difficult time concentrating on these business matters, it is of course essential that you do what needs to be done. You may even find that taking care of business keeps your mind occupied with concrete tasks and may give you a reason to get up in the morning. Business and financial matters that may need attention at this time include:

- procuring the death certificate and sending copies of it to insurance companies, attorneys, banks, and so on

- notifying the Social Security Administration of your spouse's death and applying for benefits

- closing your spouse's business or wrapping up loose ends at his or her job

- selling your spouse's business

- filing medical and life insurance paperwork and collecting insurance payouts and reimbursements

- gathering paperwork for the executor of your spouse's estate

- adjusting bank accounts

- transferring investment accounts

- examining the estate and determining whether it will leave you with enough money to live on

This last task is an important one, since research shows that if you are able to maintain the standard of living you had with your spouse, you will have a much easier adjustment to widowhood (Redfoot 1987). Having to change your standard of living means an additional major adjustment.

Mary's story is one example of how finances can complicate the adjustment process. Recently widowed, Mary expected to get her spouse's annuity. He had said that he had changed the insurance policy to list her as a beneficiary. After his death, when she filed for the annuity, she was shocked to learn from the insurance company that it was not permissible to change the beneficiary, and so Mary did not qualify for her husband's annuity.

Pause for a few moments. On the next few lines, note your estate issues, for example, do you have to roll over your spouse's 401(k) plan? _____

_____

_____

_____

_____

The Death Certificate

Taking care of concrete business tasks may periodically cause you to confront the enormity of your loss. An example of this may be acquiring and reading the death certificate. The few words on this simple sheet of paper, a "ticket" that allows you access to benefits, stand out in stark contrast to what they represent—the end of an individual's entire life.

If you do not have an attorney or professional financial adviser who can advise you with regard to legal and monetary issues and paperwork, you may want to ask a friend or a neighbor for advice on how to get the information you need. One word of caution, however: When in doubt, do not complete the forms without the assistance of an experienced professional.

Again, pause for a few moments. On the lines below, write down the names of a few wise, trustworthy people whom you could call upon as informal advisers to help you make decisions or find the information you need.

_____

_____

_____

No matter how familiar you are with your spouse's estate, you will probably end up spending a lot of energy collecting information, dealing with bureaucracies, and making life-altering decisions. Even with the help of professionals and friends, you may find that you feel overwhelmed by the many decisions you have to make.

The best rule of thumb is to make decisions in lots, tackling only those decisions that are absolutely necessary right now and deferring other decisions until later, when you are better able to handle them. Use the chart below to group the decisions you need to make, categorizing them according to the time frame in which they need to be made—short-, medium-, and long-term.

Decisions that need to be made over the next month:

1. _____

2. _____

3. _____

4. _____

5. _____

Decisions that need to be made over the next eight months:

1. _____

2. _____

3. _____

4. _____

5. _____

Decisions that need to be addressed in the next three years:

1. _____

2. _____

3. _____

4. _____

5. _____

The contents of these lists may be fluid. That is, any decision you feel comfortable making may be moved from the medium- or long-term list to the short-term list. As each decision becomes a less onerous task for you, move it to the shorter-term list.

However, you are encouraged not to make a major lifestyle change for at least two years. Why? Usually an individual's capacity to make decisions after a major loss may be compromised for a while, particularly if he or she is operating on automatic pilot.

Now that you have categorized your decisions, you can begin making them, starting with those in the short-term category. The rule of thumb at this stage of the journey is to tackle just one small decision at a time. Once you have accomplished that goal, you may take on another decision or project. For many people, just getting through the day is the only project they can handle at first. Accept yourself where you are in the adjustment process and give yourself some leeway for tackling your medium-term projects and decisions.

Your Decision-Making Process

As you adjust to your new life you will need to make a myriad of decisions about many different things. How do you go about making these decisions? The following process will be useful for you throughout your journey.

For example, suppose you were considering selling your house. How would you go about making the decision? Follow the steps outlined below.

1. Assess your current situation.

    a. What purpose has your house previously served?

    b. Now that your spouse is dead, does the house continue to serve your needs?

    c. Would you prefer a different type of living quarters (such as an apartment, condominium, townhouse, or smaller house)?

2. What is your time frame for making a change?

3. If you are considering moving, what area would you like to move to (for example, the same city, another community in the same region, or another city)?

4. How will finances affect your decision?

5. Now that you have viewed your options, do you feel you want to make a change now or defer it to a later time?

The preceding is a solution-focused process for decision making. It may be generalized to other problem-solving situations, and so you will use it frequently during this journey. So you can easily refer to this process in the future, you may want to mark it with a bookmark or fold down a corner of the page.

Please remember one thing: There is no absolute right or wrong decision in most situations. Rather, it is usually a question of one choice being a better option than another at a given point in time. Only through making mistakes will you learn and grow, so take a risk and make the best decisions you can.

Now, look at you short-term list and pick one decision on which to focus—whichever decision seems to be the easiest to address. Using the process given above, work on making that decision. As a result, you will feel empowered and more energized to tackle the next decision.

YOUR ADJUSTMENT PROCESS

Many variables may affect your particular adjustment process and the options you may have. Awareness of these variables may help you make better choices.

Some of the variables that will affect your adjustment are your age (Gallagher, Peterson, and Thompson 1981), your health (Wan 1984), and your developmental stage in life (Elder 1994). Other variables include your support systems, namely family and friends (Kalish 1982; Dean, Kolodny, and Wood 1991; Stroebe et al. 1996). Studies have indicated that friends are less judgmental than family support systems over the long run. Family supports may be helpful in the initial transition period, but they may also have a vested interest in your choices and decisions. In general, friends tend to be more stable and dependable.

Still another variable is the number of roles you play (George 1993). For example, are you a parent, a child, a friend, a mentor? The more roles you play, the easier the adjustment will be. Why? Because you can fall back on roles other than that of spouse to focus on until you are more able to accept your spouse's death and start to move on with your own life. This was a blessing in disguise for Shirley.

When her husband died, she had three small children and a part-time nursing career. She found that it took all her time and energy to manage the children and keep up with her job. She fell into bed at night exhausted. She had no time, energy, or inclination to think about anything but what was right in front of her. As a result she was able to focus on everything but herself until she gained some perspective on her husband's death. Later she could address her own personal change.

However, the two most significant variables that affect your adjustment are your capacity for resilience (Rutter 1987; Campbell, Swank, and Vincent 1991; Carstensen and Freund 1994) and your financial position in relation to what it was prior to your spouse's death (Redfoot 1987; Morgan 1980). If your financial position remains stable, your adjustment should be smoother than it would be if your financial position changes. Having financial stability gives you one less change about which you need to worry. Thus, you have less pressure to make major lifestyle changes before you are ready.

The following exercise may help you identify the variables that will have a significant impact on your adjustment. Fill in the answers below, and feel free to jot notes in the margins.

1. Age

    a. How old were you when your spouse died? _____

    b. How old was your spouse? _____

2. Health
   How is your health?

    a. Good _____

    b. Compromised _____

    c. Poor _____

3. Stage of Life
   What developmental stage were you in when your spouse died?

    a. Early adulthood (ages 20–35) _____

    b. Middle adulthood (ages 36–60) _____

    c. Late adulthood (ages 61–85) _____

    d. Late late adulthood (ages 86–100) _____

4. Support Systems
   Who makes up your support network?

   a. Family members _____

   _____

   _____

   b. Friends _____

   _____

   _____

5. Roles You Play
   Check off the roles you play in your daily life.

   _____ Wife/husband

   _____ Mother/father

   _____ Daughter/son

   _____ Employee/employer/business owner

   _____ Friend

   _____ Mentor

   _____ Other

6. Your Capacity for Resilience
   Do you adjust to change easily? Examine your past. List three times you made transitions in your life (for example, when you left home for college, or when you became a parent). How did you make these transitions? Were they easy or difficult?

   a. _____

   _____

   b. _____

   _____

   c. _____

   _____

7. Your Financial Position
   Describe your lifestyle before your spouse died:

   a. Did you own your own home? _____

   b. Did you have enough income to pay your bills on a monthly basis? _____
   _____

   c. Did you have money for extras? _____

      Trips _____

      Club memberships _____

      Eating out _____

      Entertainment _____

      Movie and theater tickets _____

      Recreation _____

      Courses (educational or recreational) _____

8. Now answer the same questions about your lifestyle after your spouse died.

   a. Do you own your own home? _____

   b. Do you have enough income to pay your bills on a monthly basis? _____
   _____

   c. Do you have money for extras? _____

      Trips _____

      Club memberships _____

      Eating out _____

      Entertainment _____

      Movie and theater tickets _____

      Recreation _____

      Courses (educational or recreational) _____

Compare your overall situation before and after your spouse died.

Janice's and Harriet's stories might be useful here, since they illustrate how your financial status as a widowed person can affect your adjustment. Janice's husband was carrying an enormous debt when he died, and there was very little money left for Janice to live on. She had never thought she would have to support herself. Now, besides coping with her husband's death, she had to look for a full-time job with benefits so that she could pay her bills, and she had to sell her house. The extra burden and forced changes made the loss even more painful.

Now let's look at Harriet's story. When Harriet's husband died, he left her enough money so that she and her children could stay in the family home without worry. This offered Harriet and the children stability and continuity of place even though their lives were in flux.

In difficult situations, having information is empowering. It provides structure, reduces anxiety, and helps you know what you face as you move into the abyss of the unknown. By identifying the variables that will affect your adjustment, you have a concrete idea of what will affect your life as you make decisions and create a new life for yourself. Some of these variables you may be able to alter, and others you may not. In either case, you will be comforted by simply having the information and knowing what to expect.

THE VOIDS IN YOUR DAILY LIFE

What will be most obvious during the first days after the funeral are the voids: Your spouse no longer leaves for work. He or she no longer comes home in the evening. His or her place at the table is empty. The food in the refrigerator does not disappear as rapidly, and you do not need to shop for groceries as frequently. Anything you did regularly with your spouse, such as going to the movies, will be very hard for you to do without him or her.

The mundane activities of everyday life will cause you to become more aware of the enormity of the loss. Simple things like seeing the two cars in your garage when you now need only one emphasize the loss. Meeting people on the street and hearing them express condolences emphasize the loss, since you cannot hide behind the illusion that your spouse is upstairs, at a neighbor's house, or away on a business trip.

Where Are the Voids?

Take a few minutes to go over your daily routine. Answering the questions below will help you identify those areas in which you will experience the voids created by the death of your spouse.

1. Did you and your spouse have breakfast together? _____

2. Did you make his or her breakfast? _____

3. Did you choose to cook foods that your spouse liked? _____

4. Did you or your spouse cook dinner? _____

5. Did you go grocery shopping with his or her food needs in mind? _____

6. What foods did you buy specifically for him or her? _____

7. Did you take your spouse's clothes to the cleaners or run other errands for him or her? _____

8. Did you watch TV in the evening together? _____

9. Did you watch your programs or your spouse's programs? _____

10. Did you have social activities with people your spouse liked? _____

11. Did you go to movies on the weekends together? _____

12. Who selected the movies? _____

13. Did you go to religious services together on the weekends?

14. List several other things you did with your spouse that you may no longer do.

_____

_____

_____

_____

Go over the list above. Note the activities for which you no longer have a partner. Pick one or two of those activities—morning coffee or dinner, for example. To make it easier to handle the void in your morning routine, make a plan to meet a friend for coffee two mornings a week. To make dinnertime more tolerable, schedule a weekly dinner out with a friend, which will give you something structured you can look forward to.

Joann missed having coffee with her husband in the morning. She decided to go to a local bagel shop where people in the community gathered in the mornings before going off to work. Seeing her neighbors every morning at the bagel shop helped her feel less isolated.

Spirituality

Many people find religion very comforting to turn to after the death of a loved one—particularly an anchor. A higher power can serve as a comforting substitute anchor or protector especially during the chaotic period following a loved one's death.

If you are religious, you may find that your religious organization offers ways for people to find solace in prayer or services. For example, in the Jewish religion, the first year after a person's death is considered the official period of mourning, during which a kaddish prayer is said as part of a daily ritual. The kaddish focuses on the living and continuation of life, not on the dead. Thus, while a person participates in the official mourning practices, he or she is encouraged to look toward the future. Around eleven months after the spouse's death a ceremony is often held in which the tombstone is officially unveiled. Although this ceremony is more of an informal custom rather than a religious requirement, it gives the mourner permission to go forward with his or her life.

Spirituality that is not connected with an organized religion may also be comforting to you if you don't belong to a church or temple and prefer not to follow a set doctrine. One woman told me that after her husband died she put aside fifteen minutes every morning to read something that had meaning to her in relation to her late spouse. Sometimes she read poetry by poets they had enjoyed together, and other times she read prose, particularly writings about nature and its beauty. She found that her "reading period" provided structure to her mornings, gave her a feeling of peace, and allowed her to continue the rest of her day with a sense of purpose and internal strength.

Whatever works for you, use it. One woman, recently widowed, came to see me for therapy. After our one session she called and said, "I do not need therapy. I found God and I'm using him to help me through this initial adjustment period."

God for this woman took on many of the characteristics she had seen in her husband. Ascribing to the anthropomorphic concept of God, she was able to find spiritual protection in a form she could accept, which allowed her some semblance of solace and peace.

So take a moment and think about spirituality in your life. Does it have a role? Could it have a therapeutic place in your life at this time?

Therapeutic Support Groups

You may find it useful to join a support group, since knowing you are not alone in your experience and being able to hear other people's stories may be comforting. On the other hand, everything depends on the group and its members—whether they are of the same generation or mixed. Attending a group made up of both older and younger widows and widowers is truly a different experience from attending a group whose members are in your age group. Josie, age thirty-six, with three young children, is in a different place than Willa, age seventy-five, with grown children.

Many support programs are offered by hospice groups. You may ask your funeral director or community family service agency for specific names and numbers of other support groups. However, it is important that you carefully investigate a group before you decide to join. The following list offers questions you may want to ask about the group to help you decide whether it is appropriate for you.

1. *Who is the leader of the group, and what is his or her background—both personal and professional (including training and personal experience)?* You may want to know that the group leader has the appropriate credentials to lead the group. Perhaps the person is an RN, counselor, social worker, psychologist, or physician.

2. *Who are the members of the group and how are they selected?* It may be helpful to know what types of participants are in the group and whether you have things like age or gender in common with them.

   Are they in your developmental life stage? Are the participants in your same stage of life? For example, if everyone in the group is in their seventies and eighties and you are in your fifties, will that be a useful group for you? Can retired people relate to your issues as a person who has to work, take care of children, and take care of household management issues with no downtime? Some diversity may be useful, but if you cannot identify with group members, the value of the program will be diminished.

3. *What are the goals of the group?* It is important to know what the purpose of the group is and whether it might serve your needs.

4. *What is the length of the group?* You'll want to find out if the duration of the group is limited or open-ended and, if it is limited, whether the group can be extended. Do you want to go to a group for a short time, and then have the group end? It may just become another loss for you.

5. *Are you committed to the full length of the group if you do not find it appropriate for you?*

Answers to the previous questions may help you decide if you want to join the support group or not.

Alice, age forty-five, joined a widows' support group after her husband died following a very brief illness. She had had little time to adjust to his illness, let alone his death. For this reason she thought the support group, held in a women's resource center in a local community hospital, would be helpful.

The group did turn out to be helpful. In fact, the group members developed meaningful relationships and found themselves looking forward to the meetings. Unfortunately, at one point the group leader heard the group laughing; she said to the women that their laughter showed they were happy again and were healing, so they obviously they did not need the group anymore. The group leader inappropriately and prematurely disbanded the group.

The group members were shocked. After getting over the initial shock of being terminated, they quickly regrouped and decided to continue meeting on their own, once a month, in members' homes. They did not have a formal leader, but by this time it had become a social support group, so they did not need a formal leader. This arrangement continued for years. In fact, a decade later many of the women still keep in touch.

With a decrease in funding, many community service agencies have had to restrict services, so there are limited numbers of support groups available. Sometimes they last only six weeks, barely enough time to get to know the members and feel comfortable enough to reveal intimate feelings. Many of these groups are called "grief groups." You may find that the emphasis on grief issues may be more than you want at this point. You may want a support group to help you as you move on with your life, not just to cope with the sadness over your loss. Remember, grief is a part of mourning, and grief and mourning are just a piece of your life transition journey.

A NEW ROUTINE EMERGES

In time, a new daily routine emerges. You find a certain level of comfort in knowing that there is some semblance of order in your changed environment. How much time does this take? For some it is a few months; for others it is a few years.

After Carmen's husband died she knew had to get on with her life—at a minimum she had to get up every morning to get her children off to school. After she dropped them off at school, she came home and got into bed until it was time to pick the children up. Parenting her children defined her role and activities and gave structure to her day. After eight months, Carmen said to herself that she could either remain a widow for the rest of her life or decide to get on with her life. She decided it was time to open her eyes a little and face a new and changed world.

Alice's experience was different from Carmen's. Alice, who had recently finished a master's program, had to complete her social work internship in order to receive the credentials she needed to begin practicing. Her youngest son had left for college so she no longer had anyone at home and could now attend to her own needs and finish her training. So she focused on her work and began exploring new activities to fill her nonwork time. Alice, an only child, did not find it difficult to be alone—in fact, at this time her experience as an only child was her ally.

Jack, on the other hand, was devastated when his wife died just six weeks after being diagnosed with a terminal illness. His wife had run every aspect of his home life. He traveled for business and was frequently gone for long periods of time. Jack had depended on his wife to take care of things at home—their two children, the house, and the bills.

Much to his surprise, Jack made some major adjustments fairly quickly and easily. Jack arranged with his boss, who was kind and accommodating, not to go on long trips for a while so that he could get his son off to college and be there to care for his teenage daughter. In the process, he got to know her better and learned how to parent her. Neighbors helped provide support for Jack's daughter when he was gone. With these adjustments made, next Jack had to figure out what kind of life he was going to establish for himself.

In the months after his wife died, Louis kept himself together by going out with coupled friends. After the unveiling, a Jewish ritual to unveil a tombstone, which frequently takes place eleven months after the death of a spouse, six people each gave

Louis the name and phone number of a woman to call for a date. Thus, the unveiling marked the formal end of one chapter in Louis's life and the beginning of another.

Pause for a moment. Think about your life since your spouse has died. What activities or endeavors have you engaged in to help you get through this adjustment period? Perhaps you've focused on caring for your children, devoted yourself to your studies or work, volunteered at a charity, or spent time with friends. Write these activities on the following lines.

_____

_____

_____

_____

_____

_____

SUMMARY

The major task of the treading water stage is to put one foot in front of the other and wait for the environment to stabilize so that you can attend to personal change in your journey. In time you will find that a new routine has emerged and you will be ready to enter the next stage of your transition journey.

Part II

Stage 2

Chapter 3

Pseudoequilibrium

When your spouse died your world was thrown into chaos, and you went on automatic pilot. You probably took care of only absolutely necessary issues and postponed all major decisions and changes until later. As time progressed, you began to put one foot in front of the other. Now your environment has stabilized. You may still be very sad, anxious, and uncertain about your future, but you do have a routine of sorts—maybe not your optimal routine, but nevertheless one that is somewhat predictable. You have some semblance of structure and order to your day. You are ready to enter stage two of the adjustment journey and address personal change.

Take a few moments and complete the following exercise. The purpose of this exercise is for you to see your new routine in concrete terms. You may only have a semblance of a routine, but putting it in writing will help any routine become more apparent.

1. What time do you get up? _____

2. What do you do first thing in the morning? _____

3. How do you spend your day? _____

4. What do you do about lunch? _____

5. What do you do in the afternoons? _____

6. What do you do about dinner? _____

7. How do you spend your evenings? _____

8. When and where do you sleep? If you have trouble sleeping, what do you do?

_____

9. How do you spend weekends? _____

This activity is geared to focus on key times in your day—breakfast, lunch, and dinner—when you would have normally connected with your spouse. You may have made accommodations to your loss in your daily life, as Shelly did. Friday night dinner was an important ritual for Shelly and her spouse. Sometimes they would eat together, just the two of them, and other times they would ask another couple to join them, but they would always be together on Friday nights. After her spouse's death, Shelly felt a terrible void on Friday evenings. So she made arrangements to go to a friend's house for Friday dinner, or she'd invite some coupled friends over.

How have you made accommodations to your loss at this point in your adjustment journey? Jot them down below.

1. _____

2. _____

3. _____

Comfort and Relief for Parents of Young Children

If you have small children at home, you probably found that the initial period after your spouse's death was framed by meeting the children's needs, demands, and schedules. Now a single parent, you may find that you do not have enough hands or time to do everything that needs to be done. It was comforting, albeit temporarily, to be immersed in the children's world, since you did not have to think about yourself for the time being.

However, at some point, maybe now, maybe several months or a year after your spouse's death, you'll need to take some time to focus on yourself and your own needs. You need to remember that you are important too. Unless you take care of yourself, you will not be able to take care of your children.

Eventually, you'll need to take one evening, afternoon, or morning each week as *your* time, even if you have to hire a sitter or call on a relative or friend to watch your children. It is important that you claim that time for yourself so that you don't lose your sense of self. Use that afternoon to meet a friend for lunch or get a manicure, pedicure, or haircut. Or spend time browsing a bookstore, going for a walk, or just relaxing. You will be glad later.

TASTING AND SAMPLING

Now that you understand the importance of seeking a new sense of order, you're ready to tackle the tasks of this stage. The goal of the pseudoequilibrium stage is to undergo surface change. Remember, your long-term goal is to craft a new life for yourself. Where do you begin? You start with a routine. Then you begin to address personal change. Your tasks during this stage will be to "taste and sample" new activities, to socialize, and to try new things and perhaps to date.

The first task in the initial phase of the pseudoequilibrium stage is to make one small personal change that will help you adapt to life as a single person. During this period you have the freedom to taste and sample some new activities to see what works for you, such as learning new skills, trying out a new aspect of your identity, and traveling to new places. Your task is to venture into uncharted territory. The world is your oyster, and you are probably limited only by how willing you are to take risks.

The following examples illustrate how people "tasted and sampled" new things.

A few months after her husband died, Diane looked in her closet and suddenly noticed that her wardrobe looked shabby. She felt a need for something new to spruce up her wardrobe. Diane's husband had been ill for a long time and she had not been shopping for at least a year. She thought maybe she should get a new sweater, maybe a shirt.

At this point, Diane was not even sure of the image she wanted to project. This would be a learning experience. Did she want to stick with her old look or go for a new look? If she wanted a new look, then what would it be? She decided she would start by looking at magazines to see the styles women of her peer group were wearing. No use looking at those skinny young models—it would just make her more depressed and remind her that she was twenty years older and single again. She knew that she looked more haggard and worn from the ordeal she had just experienced, so she wanted to find clothes that would help her look her best. Once she had an idea of the styles she liked, Diane went off to the store to sample what would look good on her.

Marilyn's story is another example of how people have tasted and sampled new things. A few months after her husband died, Marilyn realized she couldn't wait to buy Oriental rugs for her family room. Her husband had always insisted on wall-to-wall carpet, while she preferred Oriental rugs on wood floors. Now she could exercise her preference, at least in one room. It was a relief to be able to focus on colors and rugs instead of blood tests and treatments.

Another example is Karen's experience. She wanted to take a trip, but where? She and her husband had traveled extensively, and she did not want to go to a place that would trigger all those wonderful memories of intimate moments she had had with her late spouse. Where could she go? She recalled that she'd always loved Canada, and she and her husband had never gone there together. She decided she would look at several destinations in Canada and plan a trip.

Iris decided bridge lessons would be useful. She had not played bridge since college but she had enjoyed playing it back then, and this would give her an opportunity to have a social outlet with different partners. There were several bridge houses in her local area and bridge games were held several times daily. She would have unlimited opportunities to play, flexibility to join a game at the last minute, and guaranteed partners. She would not be beholden to particular partners or a set foursome, so she'd be able to simply stay home if she did not feel like playing one day.

Since her husband's illness, Iris wanted to avoid any mandatory commitments after all of the obligatory laboratory work, blood transfusions, and doctors' appointments that had dominated her life for so long. Bridge was just a fun outlet, and she needed that kind of existential activity for the moment, at least while she healed. Moreover, she looked forward to meeting new people through this activity.

Arnie had always wanted to take adult education classes. After his wife died, he found several programs in local universities and signed up for a course. He hoped the exchange in the class would provide the stimulation and social interaction he missed.

Sharon, who had gained weight during her husband's illness, joined a gym. However, she was unhappy with her body's appearance and did not want to dress in skimpy workout clothes. A friend suggested that she wear baggy sweats and an oversized T-shirt for working out. Sharon thought about it and realized that she *could* dress in baggy clothes if she wanted to. She also decided to treat herself to a personal training session once a month to help herself become more motivated.

John had decided to take golf lessons, thinking that the pro might introduce him to people with whom he could play. But since his wife died, John had to adjust to his new lifestyle, including the loss of his wife's income. To help himself adjust to life with one salary and to help pay for his wife's medical expenses, he decided to take a leave of absence from his country club and find other avenues for social interaction.

Several months after Jeannette's husband died, she realized that she found the mornings to be a lonely time. She wondered what she could do to give herself a distraction. One day she noticed lots of people walking around the running track and talking when she drove by the neighborhood school. She decided to join the group and walk the track in the morning. Soon Jeannette was invited to join the group for coffee after the walk. Now Jeanette had something to look forward to in the mornings so she could get her day going, and she did not feel so alone.

So now you're ready to taste and sample new activities yourself. How do you find new things to try and how do you decide which to try first? The following exercise may help you decide where to start. The exercise is long, but stick with it. List all of the activities you have ever done.

Activities List

List all the activities you have ever done.

Activities	As a Child	As a Teenager	As an Adult
Sports			
Arts/Crafts			
Dancing			
Reading			
Travel			
Clubs			

Wish List

List all activities you have ever dreamed of doing and prioritize them.

Activities	High Priority	Medium Priority	Low Priority
Sports			
Arts/Crafts			
Dancing			
Reading			
Travel			
Education			
Work			
Clubs			

Now look at the prioritized items on the second list, and list three things you most want to do below.

1. _____

2. _____

3. _____

From this last list, select one thing you wish to do that is realistically within your reach. For example, eliminate golf if you are not athletically inclined, and avoid travel to the Far East if you do not have the resources. Of those activities that are immediately accessible, choose one and make it your target activity to sample. By learning something new, you develop new competencies, empower yourself, and begin to develop a new image of yourself. Buying a new outfit is one way to do something new, but that is a static, one-time activity. Developing a new skill, such as learning to play golf, tennis, or bridge, is a dynamic process, which takes place over time. You will meet new people and most likely your skill level will improve as you practice; in time you will see yourself in a different light.

A word of caution: do not disregard activities just because you think you are not talented. New ways of teaching painting and drawing from the right side of the brain make it possible for all kinds of people to take art lessons.

Now that you have made your list, look at the activity that you wish to try. Research the resources in your community for that activity. Set a target date, and make the calls to enroll or join. The initial call is the hardest, and you may feel that you don't have enough energy to do the activity you've chosen, but just get started. Remember, you will meet people as you do the activity, and once you start you may feel your energy coming back.

Taking Risks

The following section will describe how you move forward with new adventures when you are afraid to take a risk and try something new.

Trying new things is easier for people to do when they feel safe and comfortable with themselves and with their world. It is more difficult to try new things when you are vulnerable. So how do you begin when fear consumes you?

Think back to when you were a little child. Remember something you were afraid of. How did you overcome the fear?

List three things you were afraid of when you were a child.

1. _____

2. _____

3. _____

Did you overcome those fears? If so, how? On the lines below, write about your experience confronting and overcoming those fears. Can you see any patterns in the way you dealt with them? Consider whether your methods of dealing with the fears were helpful or not helpful. Would you confront your fears in the same way now?

1. _____

2. _____

3. _____

I remember watching a young child go off to school for the first time. When he came home, he went into his bedroom and pulled the blankets up over his head. He was overwhelmed and scared by the new experience. However, returning to school the next day, and over the next few weeks and months, the child became increasingly comfortable with his new routine. He no longer came home and pulled the covers over his head. And eventually he began to smile and tell about his adventures in school.

The reason you look back to your early successes in overcoming fears is that it reinforces your capacity to be resilient and overcome obstacles. The confidence gained from these memories may help you confront major change, take risks, and make a transition.

Josie's story is a good example of how you might approach risk taking in your life.

Josie, whose husband had driven her almost everywhere, was recently widowed. She was comfortable driving short distances on local streets, but she did not think she could drive on highways or major thoroughfares. Now, without a driver, Josie was stuck. Either she learned to drive herself on major highways or her world would be very limited.

A friend offered to help Josie learn to drive on a local highway. They mapped out a section of the city beltway that seemed lightly traveled and had a short distance from one exit to the other. They selected a time one afternoon before rush-hour traffic began and they started off. At first Josie drove slowly, but much to her amazement she was able to go from one exit to the next. Then they circled the area and Josie drove the same route again. This time she was able to travel a little faster. Feeling victorious, she decided to try it one more time, and this time she drove at fifty miles an hour, a decent speed. Afterward Josie and her friend celebrated their accomplishment over a chocolate frozen yogurt.

Think of a fear you might want to overcome. Try facing the thing that you fear, taking small steps. Reward yourself for the accomplishment. Now pick another goal, and remember to reward yourself after you accomplish that goal. A reward might be a dessert, a new necklace or scarf, or something else you would not ordinarily buy for yourself. Or it could be a dinner out, a movie, or a sports lesson—something in which you would not normally indulge.

Now that you have selected a new activity, you have begun the personal change process. One word of caution: Don't make any *major* changes in your life for at least six months to two years after your spouse's death; only make changes on a small scale.

Religious Services and Activities

Religious services may also be a source of comfort and a social resource at this stage. Some religious institutions have modified their services so that they're more user-friendly and less traditional, often including uplifting music to give the service an upbeat atmosphere. A social hour may follow the service. Many religious organizations host other social activities, which you may find pleasurable. During the treading water stage, you may have been attending religious services regularly at a new church or temple in order to give some structure to your weekly routine. Now, as your adjustment continues and you are ready for social events, you may find this new religious venue a familiar and comfortable social milieu to begin "tasting and sampling." Also, this new house of worship venue does not push any old buttons from your married life since you started going to services there as part of your transition process.

Joann found that the religious service at her neighborhood conservative synagogue was very warm, welcoming, and comfortable. She went every Friday night and found that it helped give structure to her week. And when she felt ready, she started talking with people at the social hour after the service, opening herself to new social possibilities.

Ilene attended a conservative Jewish service in New York that featured dancing and joyous music. The people were friendly and welcoming, and the group was mixed. The warm atmosphere made her feel comfortable coming to this new place.

Marian started going to the church in her community once she had settled into a basic routine several months after her husband died. A little reserved when she first attended, she warmed up to the program after a few weeks. In time, she became part of the group and was introduced to some other people in the church community who had also experienced losses.

Family and Friends

Family and friends, an important source of comfort, are kind and supportive during the initial adjustment period, which may last from one month to one year. But when the one-year anniversary comes around, all except close friends will probably expect you to start finding your own way. While your family may be kind and supportive, they may also issue judgments about the choices you make. As a result, you may need to distance from family members so you can find your way with friends who won't judge you. It is important that you have a support network or people with whom you can honestly be yourself and do as you wish. Initially you may feel strange doing activities on your own, particularly those you had enjoyed with your spouse.

Socializing is one of the major tasks of the pseudoequilibrium stage. There appears to be a "honeymoon" period for young newly widowed women (usually during the treading water stage) when friends and family will include them in outings shortly after the spouse's death. However, very quickly, single young women become seen as a threat among the members of their peer group, who are not comfortable with the concept of death at such a young age (McGoldrick 1989). Also, coupled friends, insecure in their marital connections, may become less supportive of your new single lifestyle. At some point toward the beginning of the pseudoequilibrium stage you will probably recognize the need to expand your network to include single friends who are more in touch with and more understanding about the issues of being in a single social world.

In contrast, people in their seventies and eighties appear to be much kinder about including newly widowed friends in social gatherings, since dealing with death is a normal part of their developmental stage.

A NEW VIEW OF YOU

As you try new activities and new adventures you will begin to learn about yourself in new ways. You will see yourself through new lenses and from different perspectives. For example, traveling alone may be new for you. You will feel empowered merely by accomplishing that goal. Hiking up a mountain or taking a bike trip somewhere new may be a new experience for you. You will be amazed at how exhilarated you feel once you have gotten over your fear of trying something new. Choosing new travel options, different from the ones you chose during your marriage, may become another way of viewing yourself from a different perspective. Single women frequently find bed-and-breakfasts or European-style hotels more comfortable than large, expensive, impersonal hotels, for example.

As you continue in the pseudoequilibrium stage you will become more aware of the various facets of life without a spouse. The issue of meeting both emotional and physical needs will arise, and particularly the issue of intimacy as a newly single person.

The Need for Intimacy

During the pseudoequilibrium stage it is important to address the issue of how to meet your needs. It has been a significant period of time since your spouse has died. As time goes on you may become more aware of what it is to be needy—physically, biologically, and emotionally. You may become more aware of what it is to be alone. You may be more aware of the silence in your home. You may long to be touched; you may have a need for sex. How do you cope with and meet those needs? This is a critical juncture, at which you may be most vulnerable.

To get in touch with these needs, try this exercise:

Remember when your spouse was alive. What were the intimate moments you shared that are the most memorable to you?

1. Physical moments
   Example: Your spouse held your hand while you watched a movie.

_____

_____

2. Emotional moment

Example: Your spouse looked at you a certain way, which triggered a warm fuzzy feeling of closeness inside of you. Or, you read the paper together every Sunday, sharing articles with each other that you found interesting. Or, you felt intense love when your spouse spent all day in the kitchen preparing your favorite foods for dinner.

_____

_____

_____

Why is it important that you remember those intimate moments with your spouse? Admittedly, those memories of warm, intimate moments between you and your spouse may trigger intense feelings of sadness. However, it is important for your transition journey that you become aware of needs you have so that you may take steps to meet those needs. Recognizing needs, voids, and discomforts is an important part of the change process. While this book encourages you to find some measure of comfort as you make this journey, only your discomfort will motivate you to make changes in your life. We'll talk more about addressing your needs during your journey later in the book.

Moving toward Intimacy after the Death of Your Spouse

Intimacy is a feeling that emanates from a connection between two people. It is a pleasant, warm, and cuddly feeling that arises when two people are comfortable with each other and allow their protective walls and defenses to be lowered. Intimacy is an emotional connection that may grow over time. It may start with the physical and extend to an emotional connection, or it may begin with the emotional and extend to physical closeness.

Your capacity to experience intimacy is usually related to the level of intimacy you had with your primary attachment figures—your mother, father, nanny, or grandparents. Later those learned experiences are translated to your adult relationships with others—a mate, children, or even close friends.

If you did not have warm, nurturing primary caregivers, you may not have experienced much nurturing in your early years. That does not mean you do not want to be nurtured or that you do not like being nurtured. It may simply mean you have the capacity for intimacy but not the experience or the knowledge of how to get it. In that case intimacy at first may feel strange or uncomfortable, like a new suit you are wearing for the first time. In short, it's another new thing you have to get used to. Psychotherapy is one way of developing the capacity for intimacy. Through psychotherapy you may learn to understand your behavior and the use of defense mechanisms, such as putting up walls, which prevent intimacy from developing. Frequently the intimacy developed in a psychotherapeutic relationship is the model for an emotional connection, which you later translate to another relationship.

Each person has his or her own level of intimacy with which he or she is comfortable, depending on the quality and amount of nurturing received in childhood. You may get in touch with your intimacy comfort level by looking at close relationships you had when you were small and at the relationship you had with your deceased spouse. Was it warm and nurturing? Was it cold and impersonal? Did you and your spouse pay attention to what was going on in each other's world, or did you keep your activities and interests separate?

At some point in the pseudoequilibrium phase, you may want to pursue having a closer connection with family, friends, or even a romantic partner, or you may be perfectly comfortable with your current level of intimacy. However, your ability to have close relationships in the future may be affected by baggage you carry from either your childhood or marriage. To get in touch with your early memories of intimacy, try the following exercise:

Remember back to your childhood or early adulthood. Recall a few moments of intimacy between you and a parent, nanny, friend, grandparent, or other close relatives.

For example, Peter frequently talks about the intense intellectual discussions he and his mother had in the mornings before school when he was a little boy. Sometimes he would be late for school because both he and his mother had lost track of time. Later, in his adult life, Peter treasured the intense conversations he and his wife had over dinner and early in the morning. These conversations triggered warm feelings resulting from the talks between Peter and his mother when he was a boy.

Now jot down some of your memories of intimate moments from the past.

_____

_____

_____

_____

These memories from childhood may remind you of intimate experiences you had with your spouse, like the ones described below.

Amy remembered the times when she and her husband, Andrew, used to lie in bed on Sunday mornings and drink coffee. Andrew would caress different parts of her body. Sometimes the caressing would lead to passionate lovemaking, and sometimes not. As she thought about it, Amy felt the tingling sensations she used to experience as Andrew caressed her arms. She vividly remembered his fingers gently tousling her hair.

Amy desperately missed the physical touch and caress of another human being. As time passed after her husband's death, Amy realized that she had become more needy and vulnerable, and thus liable to make a poor decision about male company. She wondered how could she meet her needs as a newly single woman.

Allison knew what it was to miss the touch of another person. Her husband, who had always delighted in giving her informal, intimate massages, was now dead. As a newly single person she knew she would have to meet her need for physical touch. She examined her world and thought about what she could do. Then she noticed the ad for a massage therapist in the paper. How did she feel about a stranger touching her body? She did not know! But she thought it was certainly worth a try. She questioned some close friends. Those who had experienced a professional massage told her of the value and benefits of the therapy.

Allison got the name of a massage therapist from a close friend. She made the appointment and ambivalently waited. When she had the massage, the physical touch was just what the doctor ordered. It felt wonderful, and she felt rejuvenated. She realized that she needed to make regular appointments with this person. Getting in touch with intimate experiences from the past may help you frame the new experiences you have during your journey, so you will know what to look for as you fill the void created by your spouse's death.

Sex

How about sex? Traditionally, women were expected to suppress their sexual needs. Over the last forty years, since the inception of the birth control pill, many women have become less inhibited about verbalizing and expressing their sexual needs. But inhibitions or no, the need for sex is biologically driven, although you may or may not be aware of your need. What do you do to meet this need? The answer is masturbation. If you are an older woman, this suggestion may seem unthinkable, depending on your upbringing, value structure, orientation, and exposure to the world. If you are a younger woman who has been exposed to sex education programs, the suggestion may seem quite natural, however. And men may be nonchalant about the suggestion because our society has always encouraged men to find a vehicle for expressing their needs. Nevertheless, a certain amount of embarrassment may just automatically come with the territory, no matter who you are.

Interestingly, once I had a chance meeting with someone who, like me, had been widowed more than a decade ago. She fondly recounted the short-term widows' support group she had attended after her husband's death, led by an older widow. She commented about the session on masturbation and how valuable it was for the participants. This young widow found it very useful to have an older woman point out that masturbation is an acceptable means of meeting increasing sexual needs.

Marge was ambivalent about whether she could touch her own body, since she saw masturbation as taboo. Of course, she had had sex with her husband. But that was different. She was married and sex was expected, although the sex she and her husband had had was pretty routine, with little experimentation. Now she was alone, with no partner to meet those increasing biological needs. Did she have the courage to try to masturbate? She decided she would start one step at a time. She would caress her arms. Then she would caress her legs. She might touch her stomach. Maybe as she got brave she would touch her breasts. Only when she was more comfortable with those parts of her body would she touch her vagina and clitoris.

Masturbation is one way young people are encouraged to become more aware of and comfortable with their bodies. You too may find that it helps you become more comfortable with your body. Later, when you are experiencing sexual intimacy with another person, you may find that your self-exploration translates into a decrease in inhibition and an increase in sexual freedom and pleasure. Women have reported that masturbation in a bathtub is extremely pleasurable, and men have reported enjoying masturbation in the shower.

MOVING FORWARD

Tasting and sampling new activities and going on new adventures is fun for a while. You may find that you enjoy the newness of the activity and the adventure of uncharted territories, and you may also appreciate the fact that it distracts you from your life, which has voids now that your spouse is dead. However, in time what is enjoyable grows old and you may find yourself searching for something else. That search may lead you to face larger questions about your life: What do you want for your life in the long term? Do you dare risk dating? Do you want a new companion? Do you want a relationship? Are you ready to tackle a new relationship?

These questions represent a fork in the road, where you will make a major decision that will affect the rest of your life transition journey. In times past, widows most frequently chose to make an accommodation to their widowhood and not remarry. In Helena Lopata's (1973) landmark study of widows in Chicago, she found that widows at that time did not expect to live long lives, say another twenty or thirty years, without a spouse. They expected to die single, having kept their lives essentially the same—spending time working, volunteering, or whatever they were used to doing while married. These widows appeared to use adult children as their concrete anchor and calls on the memory of their late spouse and his decision-making style as their emotional anchor.

For those people who decide that they do not want to date, their adjustment journey appears to end here in the pseudoequilibrium stage. Those people appear to make accommodations to the loss of their spouse. They continue to taste and sample, engaging in new activities and adventures. They may move to a new home, even to a new city. However, these people do not appear to experience the internal change process or to qualitatively craft a new chapter in their lives.

People who do not remarry or connect with a significant long-term companion still use the memory of their late spouse as an anchor and a basis for making decisions as they remember and call upon their spouse's reasoning process to inform their own. On a day-to-day basis they may actually utilize several concrete anchors such as adult children, pets, good friends, or work colleagues, but their stable base appears to remain the memory of their late spouse.

Of course, there are exceptions and variations to this theme. Also, there are no right or wrong choices in this process. Do whatever works for you. To find out where you are in the process, pause for a few moments and jot down the name of your anchor at this point. Do you still refer to your late spouse's way of thinking when making a decision? What other anchors do you have?

1. _____

2. _____

3. _____

There are several possibilities you may choose from as you move forward. The first choice is to decide not to remarry or find a new sexual companion. In that case you will most likely maintain your connection to your late spouse and his or her memory as your anchor. A second option is to choose to date, or even develop a significant relationship, but not remarry. The third choice is to date, meet another partner, develop a relationship, perhaps marry, and integrate your lives together, blending households and children. In this case you will create a qualitatively new life with your new companion (Lowenstein, Landau, and Rosen 1994; Landau 1991).

Those women who decide to date, enter a relationship, and perhaps experience the internal dynamic growth process will establish a new chapter in their lives where their new spouse becomes their anchor and thus their new frame of reference. In contrast, men who choose to date and successfully connect with a new partner may start a new chapter in their lives, but without experiencing the internal personal change process, since men generally do not define themselves by their relationships (Gilligan 1982; Josselson 1997). I'll discuss this further in chapter 5. Thus, the journey continues. Now, I will explore the process of dating and having a relationship after a spouse's death.

Chapter 4

Dating and Relationships

By this point in the pseudoequilibrium stage, you have developed a routine that is comfortable, at least for the time being. You have begun to explore new activities and made a few small changes in your life as you are learning to live without your spouse. In this chapter we'll talk about the decision to date (or not date), the difference between dating and being in a relationship, and the role of dating and relationships in your growth process. We will also discuss dating at different developmental stages of life.

TO DATE OR NOT TO DATE

Deciding to date is a major decision. How do you decide when it is time to start dating? There is no magic moment. It is time to start dating when you decide the time is right, or when you decide something is missing from your life, you are bored with tasting and sampling new activities, and you want to expand your horizons. Or it might be time to start dating when your friends tell you that they know of someone who might be right for you. Simply put, it's time to start dating when you want companionship.

There should be no pressure to date other than that which is self-imposed; you may just decide that dating is not for you. If you do start to consider dating, you may find that you feel guilty and disloyal to your late spouse's memory. Family members may also give you some negative feedback when you mention dating. They may wonder if your spouse has been dead long enough, or they may not be prepared to hear about that part of your life. However, the decision to date is yours alone and only you must be comfortable with it.

Some women describe dating as akin to entering a lion's den. Admittedly you are placing yourself in a situation where people will meet you and decide whether they want to see you again. You are opening yourself up to being rejected at a time when you are vulnerable. On the other hand, the people you date are most likely vulnerable also, especially if they, too, are reentering the dating game.

If you've decided you'd like to try dating, you're undoubtedly wondering how to get started. The following section will give you an overview of how to enter the dating scene.

THE DATING PROCESS

Think back to the time before you were married. Remember the process of dating? You are going to return to that process, which is an unusual feeling. You have the wisdom and experience of having been married, yet you are going to go back to an activity that you haven't done in many years. Women ready to venture out on their first date often report reexperiencing all the feelings of being young again. Although they have been married, they note that they are getting in touch with new feelings about being a sexual being. And feelings of uncertainty about how they will be viewed by the other person may surface. Are they attractive? Will they be interesting to another person? Men are often concerned about two things when dating: being rejected, and being sexually acceptable to their date. As they age and their physical prowess begins to ebb, many men are concerned about their adequacy.

Pause for a moment. Think back to when you were single and recall the people whom you dated. List a few of them below.

_____

_____

_____

_____

Now reflect on how you approached those dates. What were the issues of the moment? Can you remember how you felt as you were preparing to go out on the date? Do you remember why you dated that person?

You may even find yourself smiling as you compare the feelings you have now with feelings you may remember having from the past. Is there any way you can use what you learned then about dating as you prepare to start dating now?

How to Meet People

So you're ready to date. Where do you begin? Read on for ideas.

Social Networks

The traditional way of meeting and dating is through the "traditional women's network." In past generations when women were at home or did volunteer work and men were the head of the family, women developed informal networks to communicate and gain information. In general it appears that women, by their biological makeup, are wired to be the social animal of the family. Women frequently act as the central switchboard. They make social dates with each other, seek out playmates for their children, and in general keep everyone connected. Similarly, women are often the ones who connect single women to eligible men. In story after story, I am told of a woman calling a man and giving him the name and number of an eligible woman, or of a woman working on matching eligible women with single men. This women's social network is a resource that can be called upon even today, but it is not always understood or valued by young people these days.

Of course, the traditional word-of-mouth method takes time and energy. It you're interested in meeting someone this way, spread the word amongst your women friends that you are available. Chances are, if you are patient, your friends will soon come up with someone they think might be a good match for you.

Here are two examples of how the traditional women's network works.

After Louis's wife died, he was adamant that he would never remarry. He spent his weekends playing golf with his male buddies and joining his coupled friends for dinner afterward. He told himself that he was happy and content.

But at the one-year anniversary of his wife's death, six different women handed Louis the name and number of the same woman, suggesting that he call her. He debated the situation, and then, hesitantly and with friendly female encouragement, he decided to ask Annette out. He and Annette dated and established a relationship, and later established a permanent bond. Louis changed his mind about remarrying and became engaged to Annette six months later.

Lila's story shows that, like most things in life, the traditional networking method isn't infallible. Lila had been recently widowed, and she got a call from a family friend. He asked if she was interested in dating and if he could give her number to a friend of his, Harry. Flattered that this man had thought of her, Lila said that she was available. Harry called Lila and asked her out. She accepted, and they went out for breakfast in a trendy restaurant. Harry knew he was Lila's first date. He empowered himself by becoming a self-appointed mentor to Lila and describing to her what the dating world was like. At first, Lila did not mind Harry's approach, thinking that it was an interesting icebreaker. Lila became offended, however when Harry asked if she wanted to see his bachelor pad. Internally she panicked, but she kept her cool and quickly shortened the date. Harry continued to call Lila, even suggesting that they have sex. Lila felt cheapened by this kind of conversation and let Harry know that this kind of dating was not something she was interested in pursuing.

Now, list all of the female networks you know of in your community—your book club, your children's teachers, and your circle of friends, for example.

_____

_____

_____

_____

In some cultures an appointed person will act as the designated matchmaker for the community. This matchmaker idea is again resurfacing in the United States, in more popular forms. Young and old are turning to professional matchmakers, or dating services, when their own social networks don't produce any suitable dating partners.

Activities and Social Gatherings

You can also meet people by going to singles events—dinners, dances, and parties. You may find out about these events from friends, the Internet, or singles columns in community newspapers. Going to bars with another single friend is something you may choose to do, but I do not find the bar experience a useful and productive way of meeting people with substance and character. College alumni networks often connect people who move from one city to another and are looking for a way to meet others.

Other than word of mouth, the Internet, bars, and alumni groups, how can you meet someone to date? Try an activity like golf, tennis, bridge, travel, or classes. The activity becomes the bond that can foster the new connection when you meet someone you like.

Other kinds of activities that are useful are outings that foster connections through the activity itself. Examples may be hiking, biking, and mountain climbing trips, painting trips, cooking classes, art tours, and walking tours. Attending classes and events offered by colleges and universities is a good way to meet people who share your interests. In addition, elder hostels provide many opportunities for travel, learning, and meeting others.

Janice decided to expand her social horizons through travel, hoping to meet a possible romantic partner, or at least a new friend. A friend encouraged her to take a trip with the Sierra Club, and she liked hiking, so she decided to do a hiking trip in Yosemite National Park. Her late husband had never gone hiking with her, so no old memories would be stirred up for her. Moreover, it was likely that she would meet people with whom she could make a connection beyond the trip, since Yosemite was not far from her home.

Janice found the trip exhilarating and the people interesting and fun to be with. She used her new camera and took beautiful pictures. Because it was a hiking trip, fashion was not an issue, and since supplies were packed in she didn't have to worry about carrying anything but water. She was amazed at how much she liked even the daily hiking.

At the end of the week Janice had made two new friends who lived in nearby cities. One was a single woman, Sarah; the other was a single man, Lee. From their experience on the camping trip, Janice felt that she and Sarah could travel well together in the future. Also, Janice and Sarah made an agreement with each other: Sarah would look in her community for eligible men for Janice to date; in turn, Janice would look in her community for eligible men for Sarah to date.

The male friend, Lee, was a good connection. Lee said that he often traveled to Janice's hometown on business, so Janice suggested that they have dinner sometime. Janice did not see him as good date material, but she valued the connection as a way of getting to know more about herself, and about her interactions with men as people and not just as sexual objects. By the time the trip ended, she felt it had been a great success. She had had a good time, made some new connections, and created possible future social opportunities. Janice felt empowered.

Another example of connecting through an activity is Emily's story. Emily, who loved to cook, wanted to take cooking classes in her community, but she could not find any. She got on the Web and found some nearby cooking schools. She found one that looked promising, signed up for a weeklong program, and went off to cook.

At the program Emily met Vince, who also loved to cook. Emily and Vince worked well together, and they became cooking partners at the cooking school. Emily learned something valuable from this experience: to be with a man in a capacity other than just dating, which also taught her something about herself—she saw herself as a partner in an activity, not merely as a sexual object. Emily found this to be a useful growing experience.

Barbara's experience on a trip was another interesting way to foster a connection. Barbara was divorced, and she was looking to meet someone with whom she could have a long-term relationship and possibly marriage. Barbara decided to go on a tour of Europe and Israel for three weeks. She and one other person were the only single people on the trip, but she met a married couple, Sherman and his wife, Elizabeth, who was battling breast cancer, and the three of them became friends. After the trip was over, Sherman and Elizabeth invited her to have dinner at their house on several occasions. A few months later, Elizabeth died.

Barbara wanted to connect with Sherman, but only two months had passed since Elizabeth's death, and she felt she needed permission to call him so soon after his loss. As she told me the saga of the trip and her post-trip dinners with Sherman and Elizabeth, it became apparent that Elizabeth had actually given Barbara and Sherman permission to connect after her death. I encouraged Barbara to initiate the connection.

So Barbara asked Sherman to play a game of golf with her, and after that they saw each other frequently and began a full-fledged romance. The following fall Barbara and Sherman became engaged and married shortly thereafter.

The most important thing to remember about all of these stories is that if you want to find a new mate or expand your social circle, you must be proactive. Do not sit around and wait for someone to call you. You may find that if you are not proactive you will wait for a very long time before someone calls you for a date. Get busy with a new activity. Find ways of meeting new people, who will in turn connect you with other new people. The process of networking is what is important, and it is effective. Good luck!

The Internet

One relatively new mode of networking is the Internet, where you may meet people through special interest groups or through dating Web sites. However, I find the Internet to have mixed value as a dating resource. Several dating services have proven very useful for certain age groups—people with character and substance have been able to connect, but you need to use dating sites with caution and prudence.

Some sites are self-selective, such as www.rightstuffdating.com, a site for those who attended Ivy League and other prestigious schools. Having attended a particular school does not ensure character and substance in the individual, but it does establish a common intellectual ground. More general dating sites include www.match.com and www.eharmony.com, while www.jdate.com is geared toward Jewish people.

The Internet can be a useful communication tool for dating. It allows you to get more comfortable with talking to new people, and it may give you a way to identify those qualities in another person that are important to you and those things about yourself that you may be willing to share. Also, once you meet someone interesting online, you may be able to extend the communication via the Internet for a while so that you can get to know the person a little before you agree to meet in person.

Proceed with caution when talking to or arranging a face-to-face meeting with anyone you connect with via the Internet. The Internet is a blind medium—anyone can tell you anything, and you can never be absolutely sure that the person you're talking to is telling you the truth about him- or herself. Sociopaths can be smooth manipulators, seeming to be trustworthy and honest when they're actually out to take advantage of you, either emotionally or financially.

So protect yourself: before you divulge any personal information or meet him or her in person, see if you can find a way to check him or her out. For example, if you know someone who works at the same company or lives in the same town as your online acquaintance, ask whether he or she can find anything out about this person. If he or she seems to check out, then you might consider meeting in person. The first few meetings should be in a well-lit, neutral, public setting—*not* at your home, the other person's home, or any other private setting—and you should come and go in separate cars. Don't give the person your address or any other personal information until you are absolutely sure about him or her. Always act with your mind and not your heart.

When experimenting with dating Web sites, take your time and go slowly, at the speed that's comfortable to you. You can choose to use these sites merely for practice in communicating with new people of the opposite sex—you do not have to date the people you talk to on the computer. Having a conversation can be a learning experience. Jot down what you learn just by "talking" with someone on the Internet.

Select one or two Internet sites, and look at profiles of people who seem appealing. Choose one person and practice talking to him or her, and then use the lines below to jot down the following:

Your reaction to the members' profiles: _____

_____

_____

Sites that seem appropriate for you: _____

_____

_____

Your reaction to the communication process: _____

_____

_____

Support Groups

I frequently hear about people going to support groups and making a romantic connection with another person in the group. However, these connections usually just fizzle out in time, leaving the people to wonder why they got together in the first place. The common bonds are neediness and vulnerability as a result of the death of a spouse, and the intensity and intimacy of the group were what sparked the relationship. So, do not look to your psychotherapy or support group for a person to date. Use those groups as temporary emotional resources and growing experiences.

A Red Flag

A word of caution: When you first start dating, you are needy and vulnerable (and so may be the person you are dating, since people appear to connect when they are on the same level of emotional development). You have just been through a very difficult experience. Your initial dating should be casual because you have a lot to learn about yourself and how you operate in a relationship at this point in time. Thus, your first few dates may be one-time dates—you may not go out a second time with the same person. Do not fret about what was wrong with you. Be patient. Eventually you will meet someone with whom you click and the dating will continue until you have a stronger, more predictable connection and you begin to count on each other, giving you the opportunity to see the "speed bumps" and assets in the relationship.

Older People and Dating

For this group, the dating process has a quality that is usually different than the dating process for younger men and women. Older people are aware that their life span is short. Dating and finding companionship is almost a defense against being alone. It usually does not have the same goals that dating might have for a younger population, namely marriage, sharing the same household, and blending families.

With people living longer today, many men and women end up living alone longer than they were married. Also, distance from family of origin or adult children increases older people's needs to reach beyond their family for companionship, support, and emotional connectedness. It appears that many elderly people are developing extended families and friendships instead of seeking new spouses, so they can help each other in times of need and provide a cushion against loneliness and isolation as they age.

In many of these arrangements, two significant friends help each other in daily activities but don't necessarily live together. The couple may spend a lot of time together during the week, helping each other with grocery shopping and doctor visits and enjoying social outings together. When one is sick, the other may serve as a major support. However, unlike in marriages, the partner does not play a part in all major decisions. The responsibility for making life-altering decisions when the partner is unable to do so himself or herself may remain with adult children.

Thus, for men and women in their seventies and eighties, companionship with a member of the opposite sex is what they are seeking. However, they do not have the time or inclination to experience the internal growth process, and they are not looking to start again and integrate all aspects of their life with someone new. As a result, people in this age group continue to use their adult children and their late spouse as their anchor for decision making. Rona's and Julia's stories provide useful examples of this kind of scenario.

Rona's story is an illustration of an older widow seeking companionship. Rona's second husband died after a long illness when she was in her mid-eighties. After he died, Rona was exhausted, and it took her a long time to recover. But after the first year, Rona was ready to date, and around that time she met Alan, who was great company for her. However, Rona was older than Alan, and she worried that he would not stay with her because of her age. She needn't have worried, though, because when Rona developed some medical issues, Alan was right by her side. She was so grateful for the connection and support, Rona overlooked the concerns that made Alan a less-than-ideal long-term partner. Instead, she treasured Alan's company and the support he gave her in her time of need. As she healed, she in turn cared for Alan. Instead of looking at the arrangement long term, Rona and Alan are glad to have each other on a day-to-day basis.

Another interesting tale is Julia's story. Her husband had died after thirty-five years of marriage. During the ensuing years, Julia dated a little but found it too difficult to adapt to other men's ways after being used to her own and her husband's ways for so long. She decided she would not seek to find a new partner.

However, Julia found out eleven years after her husband's death that an old high school sweetheart had lost his wife. She contacted him, and as a result he and Julia became travel companions. When she described their relationship to me, Julia was quick to tell me that they do not even hold hands, but they have traveled through Amsterdam, Ireland, and the British Isles together. Julia noted that having someone with whom to travel is a lot of fun, their shared history making it relatively easy to connect.

After some time, Julia's friend, who did not like living alone in his big, rambling house, asked her whether he might move in with her as a boarder. Julia declined, saying that their current relationship was just as she liked it and that she preferred not to take it to a new level. Instead, Julia remained anchored to her adult children in the area and stayed involved with her grandchildren. Still holding on to the memory of her late husband, she filled her other needs for companionship by spending time with this travel buddy.

It is not uncommon that women and men like Julia connect with old lovers or high school sweethearts. A shared history seems to foster new bonds more easily. Sometimes the relationship leads to marriage, but many times it does not. And sometimes people are comfortable without a companion at all.

Edward, whose wife had died five years earlier, was not interested in a relationship—he was only interested in a date for dinner or the theater, even though women called him all the time. He has a tangential relationship with his adult children and sees them occasionally, and this is sufficient for him.

As you can see, the relationship needs of widows and widowers over age seventy are quite different from those of younger people.

WHEN DATING EVOLVES INTO A RELATIONSHIP

At some point after you've been dating one person for a while (one month to about six months), the experience evolves into a relationship. If the relationship is a healthy, positive one, then you may choose to let it move forward and see what develops. If it's not healthy or it runs into differences that cannot be resolved, then the connection needs to end.

Honeymoon Period

The first six months to a year of a relationship is the "honeymoon period," when both partners feel excited about the new person in their life and are on their best behavior. After about six months, you will begin to notice your companion lets down his or her guard and is not as careful about his or her behavior as in the beginning of the relationship. Difficult issues may come up, and you may learn that you want to end the relationship. The following stories illustrate this issue.

Jim and Irene began dating. Irene looked forward to her Saturday night dinners with Jim, who was gracious and courteous at the beginning. After about six months, however, Irene noticed that Jim's table manners—a matter of great importance to her—were slipping. She was astounded by his rude behavior and decided to end the relationship.

Marlene had a similar story. Recently widowed, she received a call from a man she knew, Marvin, who asked her out. He was the first person she had dated since her husband's death two years before. Marvin was fun to be with and Marlene was enjoying the male companionship, so she stopped coming to therapy. Several months later, she called to come in for an appointment. She reported that the "honeymoon" was over, and she could not ignore the red flags that had been raised. She said she had gone on a trip with Marvin and he had behaved so boorishly that she was relieved to go to her own home when the trip was over. More recently she had gone on an outing with Marvin and he had treated her poorly. She told me that she needed to come to therapy to review what had happened so that she could end the relationship.

Edwin's is a different kind of story. Years ago Edwin and his wife and Carmella and her spouse traveled together. Many years later, Edwin's wife was diagnosed with breast cancer. She was ill for ten years before she died. Now he felt lonely, sad, and needy. After his wife's death, Edwin discovered quite by accident that Carmella had divorced her husband and was single again. He looked forward to female companionship and was delighted to discover Carmella was available.

Even though she lived in another country, Edwin felt comfortable with Carmella, and the thought of having a long-distance relationship did not faze him initially. She was familiar to Edwin, and he confused the familiarity with love. The fact that they each knew the other's family and history made their first visits smooth and comfortable. But then the logistics of dealing with work, finances, two cultures, two countries, and scheduling long-distance visits wreaked havoc with the initially very romantic connection. What was at first satisfying soon became laborious. The friendship continued, but time between visits increased, and eventually the connection just fizzled out.

Edwin's story sounds romantic and inspiring. I added it here so that you have an opportunity to observe obstacles that complicate dating and prevent its evolution to a successful long-term relationship.

How Do You Evaluate a Relationship?

As you can see from Edwin's story, not all relationship work out. So how can you tell whether a potential mate is right for you? It is in the nitty-gritty of everyday living that you can learn whether an individual is a good prospect for a long-term relationship. What are you looking for? Probably four things:

1. Compatibility of baggage

2. Compatibility of children

3. Ability to resolve conflicts

4. Personal comfort level

In this section, I will address each of these four issues. Keep in mind that each of you comes from a different background with different experiences and personalities, so hammering out a relationship with another person can be hard work.

Compatibility of Baggage

The first question you might want to ask about the connection is whether your baggage is compatible. Are you and the person you are seeing on a similar cultural plane? Are you in similar socioeconomic places? Are your religious ideas congruent? Did you live similar lifestyles in your respective marriages? Do you have similar values? Do you have compatible lifestyle goals?

Your partner's compatibility with your history is important to your comfort in the relationship. Let's look at examples of how couples have dealt with each other's baggage.

Carla was a lovely lady with an upper-middle-class background who was divorced. Her divorce had made her financially strapped, although her wealthy in-laws did provide for her children. Thus, Carla did not have to worry about the children's needs, nor would her children be a potential burden for a man with whom Carla might connect.

David was also from an upper-middle-class background. However, his wife's terminal illness had been very costly, leaving him with lots of medical bills to pay. So, when Carla and David met and began dating, they were both financially strapped, at least in the short term. They were also compatible intellectually and in their religious orientation. Furthermore, they enjoyed each other's company. Carla's and David's compatible baggage facilitated a good connection and their relationship grew.

On the other side of the coin is Sima and Harland's relationship. Sima, a widow, had been married for twenty-five years. Harland, divorced, had been married for thirty years. Sima and Harland, both new to the dating scene, were introduced by a colleague at work. Although Harland was from a different cultural background than Sima, the initial first few dates were comfortable and enjoyable. Sima was flattered that Harland continued to ask her out, and they continued to date for several months. Sima enjoyed Harland's company. She enjoyed knowing she had an outing to look forward to. She noticed she was feeling better, enjoying herself more, and relaxing. She began to let down her protective walls and experience emotions again. She had warm, fuzzy feelings she had not experienced in a long time.

All of a sudden, several weeks later, as Harland was talking about his background, Sima realized that she and Harland came from two very different worlds. He practiced a different religion. He had raised his children in a way that was different from the way she had brought up her own children. Sima realized that, although she was comfortable dating Harland, this connection could not successfully evolve into a relationship. Their baggage would not mesh comfortably. However, Sima decided to continue to date Harland, since she was not ready to cut it off.

Several weeks later, Sima noticed that what had been refreshing and enjoyable was no longer fun. She came home from a particularly uncomfortable date and realized that this connection had run its course and it was time to move on.

Another example of incompatible baggage has to do with age differences. Recently widowed gentlemen in their sixties often look to date women in their forties or early fifties. They are usually not interested in dating women who are their chronological peers. Unfortunately, age differences can pose problems in relationships.

Jason, a widower, and Joan, a divorcée, met and married when Jason was in his seventies and Joan was in her fifties. They had a wonderful relationship and enjoyed their time together. The twenty-year age difference did not matter to Joan at first. However, after nine years Jason became sick and died. Joan was devastated. She knew she might have to face the possibility of being alone the rest of her life.

In contrast, Jack dated several younger women after his wife died of rheumatic heart disease. Eventually, however, he realized that he did not want to be with a woman fifteen years younger than him. She could not relate to issues that were important to a person his age, and he could not relate to the issues of very young women. So Jack connected with a widow who was his contemporary. They dated, married, and lived a lovely life together for many years.

You can see how compatible baggage is important in fostering a new relationship. Now, think about a person you have dated with whom you had compatible baggage. Jot down three to five things that you had in common, including parallel issues—for example, you and your companion may each have two children, one of whom is very successful and one of whom is having trouble getting his or her feet firmly planted in the world.

1. _____

2. _____

3. _____

4. _____

5. _____

Next, think about the characteristics in a potential mate that are important to you. Specifically, list your characteristics alongside those of your ideal partner. Be honest; if you know that religious compatibility is of primary importance to you, then don't date someone who practices a different religion. Ending relationships is painful, and you can limit the number of painful endings by being honest with yourself at the start.

	Your characteristics	**Your ideal partner's characteristics**
Cultural background	_____	_____
Religion	_____	_____
Age	_____	_____
Health	_____	_____
Economics	_____	_____

Children's stage
of development

_____   _____

Work or
professional field

_____   _____

Political views

_____   _____

Now that you have completed this list, consider the categories in which you could tolerate differences. For example, if you are Jewish, would you be willing to be in a long-term relationship with a person of a different religion? Or, if your political views are on the liberal side, would you be willing to marry someone who has more conservative views? Write your thoughts below.

_____

_____

_____

_____

Compatibility of Children

Even if your children are grown and married and live far away, you can't ignore them. They are important to you no matter how separate either geographically or emotionally their lives are from yours. Similarly, while you do not marry your spouse's children, they may affect or significantly influence your relationship with your new spouse.

Children can create an impediment to an otherwise suitable connection. First, the financial cost of taking on a partner's school-age children may discourage men who have already put their children through college. Second, the challenges of raising children may interfere with the couple's relationship and cause irreparable damage. Furthermore, if a potential partner has already raised her children, she may not want to live with another set of children and guide them through adolescence. The following stories illustrate these points.

Barry had two teenage boys, poor students who were a handful and were always in trouble—driving fast, drinking, and hanging with the wrong crowd. In contrast, Sarah's two girls were star students, active in after-school activities and working hard to go to Ivy League colleges, where they would prepare for careers in law and medicine.

The initial dating experience Sarah and Barry had was wonderful. They enjoyed each other's company. They came from similar socioeconomic backgrounds, with similar family histories. As they continued dating, Sarah tried very hard to be sympathetic to Barry's plight with his boys, and Barry appreciated her kindness. However, in time Barry started making some sarcastic remarks about Sarah's "perfect girls." She was stunned, but the remarks kept coming—a few at first and then more during the next few dates.

Sarah decided to confront Barry about his comments. Barry denied the anger and the seriousness of his sarcasm, but Sarah knew that the difference between their children's levels of success would become a wedge in their relationship. Sarah decided to end the connection.

It is important to note that the issue here was not Barry's children or Sarah's children themselves. Rather, the issue was the impact that the children's successes had on the parents' self esteem and the carryover into the newly developing relationship. In short, Barry was using his children's success as a measure of his own self-esteem and comparing his children's achievements to those of Sarah's. If Barry had been able to relegate his boys' poor behavior to the background and allow Sarah to help him reframe the chaos into a more stable situation with the boys, Sarah and Barry might have been able to ride out the storm and develop a loving and growing relationship.

Theresa had two children, a boy and a girl. They had their faults but were both good students, active in school and community activities. They looked forward to their college experience and moving on with their futures. Sam also had two self-motivated children, who were older than Theresa's. One was in college and one had just graduated from college and was thinking about going to graduate school. Although they were older, he knew his children would enjoy Theresa's children, and that they would probably have a good rapport, with little competition between them.

Theresa and Sam both realized that their children would mesh together and that blending their families would even be fun. Theresa and Sam did not need to worry that their children would negatively impact their relationship.

Remember Carla and David? They each had a college-age child who had had difficulties and was struggling to find a sense of self. Naturally, David was sympathetic to Carla's daughter's plight, and Carla was supportive and helpful regarding David's son. So David and Carla had compatible baggage, compatible children, and a desire to support each other through tough times.

You and your children are connected, and with any future relationship you should consider the compatibility of your children because of the possible negative impact on that relationship. You will be more likely to have a successful match if you have similar approaches to handling difficult questions and financial issues with regard to children. There is no right or wrong approach; what is important is the compatibility of your methods of resolving conflict and your persistence when handling difficult issues. And, the older and more financially independent the children are, the greater the likelihood that children and their issues will not negatively impact your newly formed relationship, because they will present fewer problems for you to solve together.

Consider any three issues related to your children or your companion's children that may present challenges to your relationship with him or her. Jot them down below.

1. _____

2. _____

3. _____

Look at your newly formed relationship. Are there areas of tension building about the children? Does either partner have unrealistic expectations regarding children? Write down your feelings about this tension and any ideas you have about how to work out the problem with your partner.

_____

_____

_____

Remember, you are your companion's partner, not the stepparent of his or her children—until the children accept you as such. You may be another adult in their world whom they have to respect, but they do not need to see you as a parent.

Extended Families

Children are not the only people to be considered. Families of origin can have a profound impact on a relationship.

In Arnold and Carrie's relationship, their children were not the problem. The difficulty came from Arnold's sister, who was severely learning disabled and in denial about her disability. Carrie believed that Arnold, out of guilt, was letting himself be manipulated by his sister, who refused to comply with medical advice that would help her become self-sufficient. Carrie was concerned that Arnold would continue to be sucked into his sister's downward spiral because of his guilt. Since Carrie was the major money source in this relationship, she worried that she and Arnold would run into some serious potential conflicts and financial difficulties. Carrie and Arnold sought therapy to work on their difficulties. Fortunately Arnold began to see what Carrie was talking about and agreed to set limits on what he would do for his sister. Thus, Carrie and Arnold could successfully move forward with their relationship.

Now take a few moments and think about your extended families. Are there any issues that you are concerned about? List them below.

_____

_____

_____

Think about ways you might address the areas of conflict. Do not push them under the rug. You do not have to come up with an immediate solution to the problem, but you must begin by talking about the issue and your concerns with your new companion.

Resolving Conflict

As you see your companion more and more, you will eventually run into conflicts. How do you resolve the differences you have? Ignoring disagreements is not useful. If your relationship is to continue and succeed, it is important to find ways of compromising and resolving differences to both individuals' satisfaction. Conflict that continues to be unaddressed builds until it becomes a wall between the two individuals and communication breaks down. Thus, it is important that the couple learn early in a relationship how to:

1. Identify issues of difference and discord.

2. Figure out whether there are ways of negotiating the differences.

Resolving conflict in relationships is a perennial problem. All couples deal with this issue. Even people in sixty-year marriages will have discord.

Many times when two people start dating neither wants to make waves by making an issue out of small differences. So each person may try to ignore annoyances, such as one person always being late for dates, until they get very angry and may explode.

Here is an example:

Jeremy, a California native, had a casual style of dress, preferring to wear jeans or khaki pants, sandals, and white socks. Simone, who was from the East Coast, liked a more traditional style of dress, such as button-down shirts worn with a blue blazer or suit.

After they had dated for a while, Simone finally told Jeremy that she was uncomfortable with his dress for social occasions. Jeremy was surprised, but he asked Simone what she would want him to wear. She said she would prefer that he wear dress pants, a button-down shirt, and a tie and jacket for social occasions, but that she would be okay with him dressing in his own style for other occasions. Simone also admitted that she hated sandals worn with white socks. Even though Jeremy loved wearing sandals with white socks, he agreed to wear button-down shirts for social occasions and whatever he wished at other times.

While this conversation may sound ridiculous, the back-and-forth negotiation of acceptable dress between Jeremy and Simone is the very basis of conflict resolution couples need to learn to use, whether the topic is clothes, food, housing, or finances.

Here is another, less constructive, example of conflict resolution.

Linda noticed that Geoffrey frequently picked her up fifteen to twenty minutes late for dates. To teach him a lesson, one night she decided to make *him* wait twenty minutes after he arrived to pick her up. Geoffrey was sullen during the date. Linda asked what was wrong, and Geoffrey pointed out how late she had been. Linda commented that she was just giving Geoffrey "some of his own medicine."

Linda's approach was not a useful one. If she was angry at Geoffrey or annoyed by his lateness she needed to say it, not lower herself to his level. Geoffrey, however, was stunned by Linda's remarks. He never realized that his being late was an issue, even though he was annoyed when she was late.

As you can see, both people need to address the speed bumps that arise as the dating continues. Hoping things will improve automatically without discussion is wishful thinking—a passive exercise that is not always fruitful. Pushing the issues under the rug and not addressing them step-by-step creates a problem in an evolving relationship.

People in relationships are usually complementary. One partner may be more deferential than the other. However, it is important that the other partner gets a turn at having his or her needs met on occasion; otherwise the one who is deferential might wind up exploding one day because he or she has been giving in all the time.

Usually you carry patterns of interaction you are used to into a new relationship. These patterns of interaction may be unconscious, and many times they are learned behaviors that you have observed your parents using. Or, if you observed destructive patterns of interaction, you may use the opposite patterns. So, if your parents had intense emotional battles, you may react by avoiding all conflict or by keeping emotional distance from your mate in order to limit the level of emotional intensity. Or you might have only rational discussions about disputed issues and halt the discussion if it becomes emotional. Becoming aware of your learned behaviors is the first step toward resolving conflict in a relationship.

No matter what the conflict or your emotional style, once you are aware of the issues that are not working for you or your partner, you can discuss them so that the relationship can move forward in a positive and meaningful way. If a relationship evolves and then gets stuck, there is a reason. It is important that you determine the reason and see if you can resolve it—you can learn early on in a relationship whether a situation can improve with discussion. If you voice your concerns and the situation gets better for a few weeks but then reverts back to the original problem, you are seeing a red flag, and you must readdress the issue. If it does not improve, decide whether you can live with the problem, or whether you need to end the relationship so that you can move on and find another connection.

While there are always variations on the themes discussed above, these kinds of issues are important considerations that can help you determine whether a dating connection will evolve into a meaningful, permanent relationship.

Now let's look at the basic method of resolving conflicts.

Everyone has his or her own style of negotiating differences. Conflict resolution is not black and white—there is no right or wrong answer. The solution is the process, because the process you develop with your significant other will become a cornerstone of your relationship.

The key to resolving conflict is to problem solve until the resulting solution is somewhat satisfactory to you and your new mate. With your partner, work through the exercise below to see if you can arrive at a solution.

1. Identify the problem: _____

2. Brainstorm several possible solutions. Keep in mind that there are probably no black-and-white solutions, unless the issue involves life and death.

Possible Solutions

_____

_____

_____

3. Write down the upside and the downside of each solution.

Possible solution: _____

Upside   Downside

_____   _____

_____   _____

Possible solution: _____

Upside   Downside

_____   _____

_____   _____

Possible solution: _____

Upside   Downside

_____   _____

_____   _____

4. Prioritize options by least significant downside.

    1. _____

    2. _____

    3. _____

5. Decide which option you will use, and write it below.

_____

Try this solution. If it works, congratulations! You have successfully resolved a conflict. If it does not work, then go back to the first step and begin the process again.

This is a process that should be mutually negotiated by you and your new companion. If you're lucky, your partner will be adventuresome in working through these steps. If your partner is resistant about the process at first, try the exercise on your own. See what solutions you arrive at and then approach your partner. Remember, all new relationships have a learning curve and learning how to negotiate conflict is part of it. If, however, you can find no way to negotiate differences, you may have to consider terminating the relationship, since the ability to compromise is important for the success of a relationship.

Relationships Are Like a Seesaw

The rhythm in a relationship is like the movement of a seesaw. Like a seesaw, all relationships work to achieve a sense of equilibrium, balance, or homeostasis. Of course, life is dynamic and not static. People are frequently in flux. At any given time one person in a relationship may be experiencing difficulty in certain areas, such as work; while that person may be down, it is important that the relationship partner be stable, or even up. Having one partner be up while the other is down, allows the "down" partner time, support, and stability to regain his or her sense of equilibrium and thus helps to rebalance the couple relationship.

However, frequently when one partner in a relationship is down, the other partner also gets depressed. At that point the whole couple system is in the doldrums, so it is clearly preferable for one member of the relationship to be up when the other person is down. Establishing flexibility, rhythm, and balance is important for a relationship to work over the long run.

Comfort Level

Frequently I hear people describing someone they have met. They will tell me what he looks like, where he is from, and what he does for work. They will describe how he lives and what kind of car he drives. But only on an occasion will the individual tell me how the person makes her feel.

Only you can know how you feel inside when you're with the new person in your life. So ask yourself, How do I feel inside after being with this new person for more than a few dates? I hope that your answer is "internally peaceful." I think a relationship should provide you with a feeling of peace and contentment, particularly one that is formed later in life. It is these internal feelings that will tell you what your comfort level with your companion is.

Contentment

In my work as a psychotherapist, over the years I have found that the words "love" and "happiness" are overused. Society, individual cultures, and the media have had so much influence on the meaning of these words that people frequently have difficulty describing what these words mean to them.

I have found that it is more useful to use the word "contentment" when discussing goals to be achieved, rather than "happiness" or "true love."

Think about your life. Recall a period in your life when you felt contented.

1. What made you content? _____

2. Do you feel content now? _____

3. Do you have periods in your present life when you feel content? _____

4. If so, what makes you content? _____

5. If not, can you explain why? _____

It is meaningful for you to find both personal peace and contentment and contentment and peace in a relationship. Lets examine the difference between these two types of contentment.

"My life is wonderful," Patricia told me. "I have a wonderful husband and a beautiful new house. Yet I am not happy." I asked her why she thought she was not happy, but she did not know. As we talked it became apparent, though, that she was depending on others to give her day meaning since she stopped working. No individual can feel content when they wait for everyone else to be available. Patricia focused her day on others because she had no internal passion of her own driving her. She would wait for her husband to get home, and for others to need her. Her waiting put a burden on her loved ones, who know that Patricia is dependent on them for meaning in her life.

Patricia needed to find a way to achieve personal contentment. What I am suggesting for you as you make this journey is that you try to identify what makes you content, and perhaps look to other ways of finding contentment if the current ones aren't working.

When Gloria met Max, Gloria suddenly stopped running from activity to activity to meet her needs. Her sister commented on the difference in her behavior, observing that Gloria must feel content having Max in her life, and that perhaps her emotional needs were being met. Gloria stopped to consider what her sister was saying and realized that she was right. Gloria, already personally content with her work, was content in a relationship for the first time in her life.

Jody, a personal trainer, loves to work out frequently. But one summer Jody was so busy with her work that she had no time to work out. She started complaining about everything—she did not feel good, she had no energy, she disliked her life. Once her work slowed down Jody began working out again, and all of a sudden she felt better. Her life had not changed, but her perception of herself had, because working out was Jody's passion, which was intricately tied to her sense of self-esteem and personal contentment.

To illustrate the concept of contentment in a relationship, let's look at Josie's story. Josie was a struggling musician who hoped to do well professionally, and Jeremy was a professor at a nearby university. Josie and Jeremy dated for several months and developed a relationship. Then a speed bump arose. Josie was offered the opportunity to study abroad for six months with a famous music teacher. She was torn—her relationship with Jeremy was going well, and she didn't know whether she should risk being away for so long. So she hesitatingly discussed it with Jeremy.

As it turned out, Jeremy was thrilled for Josie, and he encouraged her to accept the offer. He told her he would come visit halfway through, and that they would talk and keep touch by e-mail. Jeremy knew that if Josie were personally happy, the chances of their relationship working and moving forward would increase. If Josie stayed behind on account of Jeremy, he knew she would harbor anger at him later on. So Josie went abroad for six months, and she and Jeremy continued their relationship long-distance. Upon Josie's return from Europe, she and Jeremy began making permanent plans for their future together.

So what is your passion? How do you define contentment? Jot down some notes below regarding times in your life when you have felt a sense of personal, internal contentment. What contributed to that feeling?

Time in your life	Event(s) that contributed to your feeling of personal contentment
1. _____	_____
2. _____	_____
3. _____	_____

Next, write down your memories of times in your life when you have felt a sense of contentment in a relationship. What contributed to that feeling of contentment?

Time in your life	Event(s) that contributed to your feeling of contentment in a relationship
1. _____	_____
2. _____	_____
3. _____	_____

You are now aware of the four factors that impact the success of a new relationship: compatibility of baggage; compatibility of children; ability to resolve conflicts; and personal comfort level. Keep them in mind as you move forward in your journey.

ALL THAT GLITTERS IS NOT GOLD

In the dating phase of the pseudoequilibrium stage, you taste and sample different dating experiences. You learn about yourself in the context of another person, different from your former spouse, through these experiences. One of these dating experiences may evolve into a relationship. At first the relationship will feel like heaven and you will be pleased by its newness and healing qualities. But in time, conflicts and internal anxiety may show you that the relationship is not working. When you are tempted to deny the inevitable—the ending of the relationship—you may find the following stories useful.

Carla longed to have companionship and be held, so when she met Jerry on the Internet and went on a few dates with him, she was ready to invite him into her life and her home. But before she did, she got a friend from Jerry's community to ask around about Jerry and learned that he had been very abusive to his first wife. Carla had not noticed anything during their dates, but now that she had the information, she would proceed more cautiously. After all, this was the honeymoon period where he would present his best façade.

Here's another example: Ruth and Louis dated for several months, even moving forward into a sexual relationship. Occasionally they spent the night at each other's house, but they did not live together. Ruth was surprised at how easy and smooth the connection was. She looked forward to her outings with Louis. Reasonably, they talked about an immediate future together.

Then one day, seven months after the relationship had begun, the bubble burst. Louis relaxed and began to show his true self. Over the next few weeks Louis began to have small, explosive outbursts of anger that seemed to come out of nowhere and have no purpose. She noticed her reaction—a growing sense of fear and uncertainty, since she never knew when the next explosion would happen—and decided she could not permanently live this way.

She discussed her feelings with Louis, but he dismissed the impact it had on her and rejected discussing it or going to a professional for help. Ruth told him that her father had had an explosive temper, that Louis was pushing all her old buttons, and that the situation was becoming increasingly uncomfortable for her. Because he refused to acknowledge the problem, she ended the relationship.

Several months later Louis called Ruth to see if she would be interested in trying again. Ruth said no. She had learned that the only gain would be a few fun dates and then the old explosive angry outbursts would rear their ugly head again. Pleasantly but firmly, she declined to see him, wished him well, and said good-bye.

When the relationship is no longer working for you, listen to your body and your head and end it. With the ending of your first significant relationship after your spouse dies, you come to the end of the second part of the pseudoequilibrium stage and are catapulted into the next process, transition to liftoff. You are now ready to go to the next phase in the journey.

Chapter 5

Transition to Liftoff

Men and women negotiate the transition to liftoff part of the adjustment journey differently. A core principle of the spousal loss model is that those women who choose to date enter a relationship with the goal of crafting a new chapter in their lives. They select a path that leads them through a difficult but rewarding process of dynamic internal growth and maturation.

As I stated earlier, those women who do not date and enter a permanent relationship with the idea of crafting a new chapter in their lives appear to have a more linear journey. They remain in the early part of the pseuodequilibrium stage, tasting and sampling new activities and making accommodations for their single life, but they do not seem to experience this internal personal growth process. The characteristic that affects the journeys of both sets of women is their anchoring frame of reference—either the late spouse, or the new spouse or partner, depending on whether the women have connected with a new partner or not (Levinson 1997). Women who have a new spouse seem to use the new permanent partner as their anchoring frame of reference; those who do not reconnect seem to continue to use their late spouse as their anchor, even forty years after their spouse has died.

Why do women and not men seem to go through this particular process of internal growth and maturation? The answer has to do with how women and men form their identity (Gilligan 1982; Josselson 1997). It appears that in most situations men form their identity from their work, while women form their identity based on their relationships (Gilligan 1982; Josselson 1997).

In my study of women whose spouses had died, I found that they identified themselves by their relationships and significantly identified their late spouse as their anchor. It appears that if a woman wants to move on with her life after the death of her spouse, have a new spouse, and a new chapter in her life, she will have to recraft that part of her identity that was defined by her late spouse. The transition to liftoff part of the journey is where that recrafting process takes place.

Transition to liftoff is a process, not a stage. It is a transition period of growth between stage two, pseudoequilibrium, which has to do with personal change on the surface, and stage three, renewal and resolution, during which an emotionally matured and changed person integrates himself or herself with his or her environment. Transition to liftoff is a period of dynamic, not linear growth (Watzlawik, Weakland, and Fisch 1974) resulting in the person leaping from one level of emotional development to another. The name of this phase, *transition to liftoff*, evokes a speeding rocket, to reflect how you move on your personal trajectory from one stage of emotional maturation to another.

THE TRANSITION TO LIFTOFF PROCESS

When you first started to date, you were needy and vulnerable and probably connected with someone who was at your same level of emotional development and thus needy and vulnerable also, although his neediness may not have been apparent at first.

As you dated this person and a relationship developed, you began to heal from the major loss you experienced when your spouse died, lowering the defensive walls that you had immediately built and experiencing the feelings of nurturing, intimacy, and sex again. In time, as you healed, what had been warm and exciting may have become less satisfying. You encountered conflicts in the relationship and became aware of issues that might make the relationship problematic for you over the long term. In time, you may have ended the relationship and as a result begun this transition process.

An example of how the transition phase is initiated can be seen in Gary and Lois's story. Gary, many years older than Lois, was flattered that she—cute, petite, and bubbly—would go out with him. Gary was kind and nurturing, and Lois enjoyed his company. She was worn out from taking care of her sick husband and she found it nice to have someone take care of her for a change. She noticed how good she felt the morning after a date. Her wrinkles did not appear so severe, her gait was a little lighter, and she smiled all day.

As Lois dated Gary, she started regaining her energy. However, the better she felt, the more she noticed the warts in the relationship. She realized that Gary was too old for her; he had plenty of energy and could keep up with her, but they enjoyed very different lifestyles. Lois allowed the relationship to continue for several more months, despite her knowledge that it wasn't working, but then Gary started making noises about moving in with Lois, and she knew she had to end the party. She told Gary that the relationship was over.

Much to Lois's surprise, she experienced great sadness at this point. Suddenly she was alone again, only now she didn't have people around to comfort her as she did after the loss of her husband. She became very depressed, which made her confused. She had dated Gary only for a very short time—why was she feeling so bad?

Well, in dating Gary and having all those good times, Lois had lowered the barriers that were protecting her ego and allowed herself to feel again. She was no longer numb and in shock. And, in fact, now that she had ended the relationship with Gary, she began to feel again, only this time it was major pain—pain from the loss of her good times with Gary, but also from reexperiencing the sadness from the loss of her husband. This pain was devastating. Now, having gained some distance from the death, Lois was able to look at the pain of the trauma she had experienced. When her husband died, she was numb and in shock and did not feel pain with the intensity that she was feeling now.

Having experienced the end of her relationship with Gary, Lois was now ready to mourn the end of this relationship—and also the death of her husband—in a way she could not during the treading water stage. With distance, perspective, and time, Lois can mourn as she is now free to feel in a way she could not earlier.

IF THE FIRST RELATIONSHIP DOES NOT END

But what if the first relationship does not end? Then you will probably not experience the internal growth process phase. (A colleague of mine told me that she had consciously chosen not to date after her spouse died because she never wanted to experience the loss of a new spouse and reexperience the kind of pain she knew after the death of her first spouse.) There are exceptions to this rule, of course. Keep reading in order to better understand the purpose of this phase of the adjustment process, its value, and your choices.

Why Change?

But why do you need a change? The answer is that your old life is over, and you are starting a new life. When you connected with your spouse you were in a different developmental place. You were younger. Your stage of life was different. Your life goals were different. Now, as a widow, you may have a career. You may have young children, or your children may be older and out of the house. The fit between you and your spouse is gone; the pieces that made your relationship complementary are over. The odds are very small that you will find a human being who will fit the space your spouse previously filled. And so you need to change in order to adapt to and grow in your new life.

THE INTERNAL GROWTH PROCESS

How does this internal dynamic growth process occur? With the ending of your first relationship after your spouse's death, you experience sadness and pain. But this new relationship wasn't in place long enough to cause a large ego insult—you were not with this person long enough to have your total sense of self or your self-esteem affected by the relationship's end. What happens is that this recent loss triggers the release of the painful feelings you may have experienced and blocked after the death of your spouse or perhaps of other major losses you have experienced in your life. You are thrust into a place where you mourn both the loss of the recent relationship and the death of your spouse.

As I discussed in chapter 2, Mardi Horowitz (1990) explains that as you get more distance from the loss of your spouse, you will develop different schemas, or pictures, of the person you lost. Time and distance serve as protective devices for your ego, and it is now safer for you to mourn the loss of your spouse. Moreover, you will mourn him or her differently than you did immediately after his or her death.

Anchorless State

The challenge in this process is that you are now without a primary anchor. You are drifting in a sea of everyday life and feel like you are in permanent limbo. Like an anchorless boat, your drifting may offer numerous new opportunities only restricted by your willingness to take risks. As long as you have your health and your zest for life, you can move forward. The anchorless state offers you the opportunity to learn how to live and be yourself on your own without a mate, accepting the possibility of not having another partner in your life. Then, if you allow another mate to come into your life in the future, it will be by choice, not necessity.

While in this anchorless state, you still may have some transitional anchors. An example may be an adult child, a pet, a parent, a close friend, or a therapist. Stop for a moment and jot down names of individuals who might become your transitional anchors at this point in your adjustment journey.

_____

_____

_____

Psychic Pain

The pain you're experiencing is called "psychic pain." Some people describe it as a pain in their chest or abdomen. Some people say that they feel they are in a dark tunnel or a deep, dark hole, as do people who are experiencing major depression. During this time, you should once again put one foot in front of the other and get through the day. It will get easier. If you find the pain immobilizing, you may want to check with your medical doctor for some medicine or seek psychotherapeutic help.

This pain, while devastating and terrible to experience, is the pain that psychotherapists address in their work, and it will serve as a catalyst, allowing you to grow internally and move forward with your life. Some people will have the energy and inclination to pursue this growth process right away, and others will be so overwhelmed by the pain of both losses that they will find themselves struggling just to cope on a daily basis. There is no right or wrong answer, nor is there a time limit. The choice is yours. You may move forward in your journey, or you may choose to tread water for a while until you feel ready to tackle this dynamic emotional growth process.

Self-Reflection

During this period you may find yourself doing a lot of self-reflection. You may revisit the relationship you just recently experienced. As you reflect, jot down what was good and what was bad in the spaces below.

What was good about the relationship: _____

_____

_____

What was bad about the relationship: _____

_____

_____

Now look in the mirror. Examine your face, your body, and your whole image. How do you see yourself both physically and emotionally? Do you look older? Are there lines and gray hairs where there never use to be? Do you look sad, numb, or emotionally worn?

_____

_____

_____

Next, ask yourself the following questions: How do you define yourself? Do you like the person you see in the mirror? If not, what would you like to change? Look beyond your appearance and look inside yourself. Write your thoughts below.

_____

_____

_____

Beginning the Internal Growth Process

"So how do I go about this change process? How do I recraft my identity?" you may be wondering. There is an inherent contradiction here: the very reason that you have the opportunity to make major change in your life is the same reason you are in pain. Your loss, the vacuum in your life, has destabilized your world and presented you with the chance to initiate the emotional change process. The pain you are feeling serves as a catalyst for change.

This dynamic change process is the major task of the transition to liftoff phase of the journey. Achieving this change is like scaling the steepest part of a mountain—the summit of the journey.

So the question remains: how do you experience this internal change process and recraft your identity? You begin by reviewing your life with your late spouse.

1. List the roles you played in your marriage.

---

2. Assess and prioritize how meaningful each role was for you, listing the most meaningful first. For example, if you liked cooking dinner each night you'd write "meal planner" or "cook" high on your list. If your special outings with your spouse were especially important to you, you might start your list with "travel companion." On the other hand, if you hated cleaning the bathrooms, you'd write "cleaning person" or "housekeeper" lower on your list of roles.

---

3. How was the marriage romantic? For example, perhaps your husband brought you flowers once a month.

---

4. Identify practical aspects of your marriage, both positive and negative. For example, maybe your spouse was a wonderful breadwinner and you never had to worry about money, or your spouse always took care of home repairs.

---

5. Identify the physical aspects of your spouse. How did you like your spouse's appearance? Describe the attributes you liked and didn't like.

_____

_____

_____

6. Identify aspects of your lifestyle with your spouse. For instance, perhaps you loved the vacations your wife planned every year, but you disliked her cooking.

_____

_____

_____

Next, answer the following questions about your recent relationship.

1. What was the relationship like? Was it like a long-term date? _____

_____

2. How did you spend your time together? _____

_____

3. What roles did you play in this relationship? _____

_____

4. How did you feel about yourself in each role? _____

_____

5. What were the rules? _____

_____

6. Who had the power? _____

_____

7. What were your expectations? What were his or her expectations? _____

_____

8. What did you like about this relationship? _____

_____

9. What did you dislike about the relationship? _____

_____

10. Were there roles that you played in your recent relationship that were similar to those you played in your marriage? List them here. _____

_____

11. Were there roles that you played in your recent relationship that were different from those you played in your marriage? List them here. _____

_____

12. If you could have changed anything about your life with your spouse, what would you have changed? _____

_____

13. What would you have kept the same? _____

_____

(Note: If you are currently in your first relationship since your spouse died and it has not ended, skip the next five questions.)

Now look at your life since your husband or wife died, apart from the relationship you recently ended.

1. How is your life different? _____

_____

2. How are you different? _____

_____

3. How have you compensated for your spouse's death? _____

_____

4. What parts of your life are the same as they were when your spouse was alive?

_____

5. What parts of your life are different? _____

_____

Finally, take a closer look at your most recent relationship. Review the roles you played while in that relationship. Look at yourself in relation to the other person.

1. How were (are) you different with that other person than you were with your spouse? _____

_____

2. How were (are) you the same? _____

_____

3. Did (does) this new companion depend on you for certain things? _____

   If so, what? _____

   _____

4. What did (do) you depend on him or her for? _____

   _____

5. Did you depend on your spouse for those same things? _____

   _____

What I am encouraging you to do is to enter into a process where you assess the reciprocity, or interrelatedness, in your marriage and compare it with the reciprocity in your recent relationship.

This reciprocity, or interrelatedness, between spouses is often seen in the way partners renegotiate their relationship in order to meet each other's needs at different points in their marriage. When you married your spouse many years ago, both of you were in a different developmental stage of life than you are now. Your needs and issues changed as you went along. Perhaps in the marriage you had the opportunity to revise the terms of your relationship to account for the changes in your life station and different needs. Or perhaps you did not. In either case, it is common that relationships formed later in life have a different interrelatedness than prior, long-term relationships. Think about your two relationships. See if you can identify the interrelatedness in each relationship by looking at your responses in the previous exercises.

Then, in the space below, jot down your thoughts about the interrelatedness in each relationship. The purpose of this exercise is to make you consciously aware of things that you took for granted in the relationships. For example, Doris had depended on her husband, Peter, to tell her about the weather and traffic conditions every morning. And Peter, who could hardly remember his own phone number, had depended on Doris to keep him informed about social engagements and maintain their address book.

_____

_____

_____

What do you do with all these notes? Examining your lifestyle and relationships helps you to see what works for you in your life and in your relationships, and what does not. It also helps you to know what aspects of your life you'd like to be different in the future.

You may look at this process as a puzzle with pieces you need to fit together, and you have to assess each piece to see where it fits. Just as you fit puzzle pieces together, you have to look at each person and examine the way he or she relates or connects to you and your life.

More Self-Reflection

In the exercise below, you will be able to gain a sense of yourself as you were in your first marriage. In previous exercises you compared your recent relationship with your marital relationship. This exercise is focused on *you* and allows you to evaluate functional aspects of yourself so that you know your strengths as you prepare to enter a new and more fulfilling relationship.

1. At what age were you married? _____

2. Did you ever live on your own before marriage? Or did you go from your parents' house to your spouse's? _____

3. Did your marriage follow a traditional path or was it a more modern arrangement? _____

4. Did you have a job or a career? What did you do? How much of your emotional energy did it take? _____

    _____

5. How did you spend the balance of your time? _____

    _____

6. How did you and your spouse spend time together? _____

    _____

7. Did you volunteer? What type of volunteer work did you do? _____

    _____

8. Did you have children? _____

9. Did you raise them? _____

10. How do you feel about your parenting? _____

    _____

Now you are at a crossroads.

1. How do you want the next chapter of your life to go? _____

    _____

2. Whom do you want to be? _____

    _____

3. How do you want your world to work? Daydream. Envision various scenarios. Understand what motivated you in the past, and whom you wish to be and what you want to do in the future. Make some notes below.

_____

_____

_____

The Dynamic Quality of the Growth Process

The growth process you are experiencing at this time is an internal personal, emotional maturation that is dynamic in nature.

It may be easier for you to visualize what the dynamic quality (Watzlawik et al. 1974) of this process means if you think about how an athlete builds skill. Let's look at a tennis player's serve, for example. It starts at a low level—he can't even get it into the serve box. Over time, though, with lessons, practice, and experience, he will learn to get it into the serve box. Later, as he matures and continues to practice, the serve will do more than just land in the serve box; it will gain speed, direction, and determination. Thus, the tennis player will serve on a different skill level than he did at first. That player will have had a growth leap in his athletic abilities. The change may be subtle or it may just occur all at once. The same is true of people's emotional growth.

Similarly, an artist who has been creating on one level for a long time may find that one day, or over the course of a year, her work just got better. What she is experiencing is an internal maturation process of her artistic skill.

It is very difficult to go through this amorphous growth process. You may feel frustrated because you do not see obvious signs of growth on a regular basis. Be patient, stay focused, and continue your self-reflection. After some time, all of a sudden you will leap forward and experience this dynamic growth. When you get discouraged, you may find it helpful to use the affirmations described below.

Affirmations

This process is slow and sometimes painful. Repeating affirmations on a regular basis can help you maintain your resolve as you work to recraft your identity. A simple affirmation may be:

"I can do this. I need to do this. I will do this."

Practice your affirmation in front of the mirror daily. It will give you confidence and a sense of empowerment to forge ahead.

To further build your confidence, think back to another time in your life that was traumatic. What resources did you call upon at that time to get through the difficult period? Would they be useful now? Write your thoughts here.

_____

_____

_____

Do You Have to Experience This Growth Process?

The answer is no—you do not have to go on this journey. The choice is yours. Sometimes people begin the process, find it too painful, and defer it for a period of time. Later, when they feel they have enough energy, or when their life is not working for them and they know they need to do something to move forward, they may resume their journey.

Unless you go through this entire change process you will experience only the initial change and make accommodations for your spouse's death in your life. You will stay in the pseudoequilibrium stage and continue to taste and sample for the rest of your life. After some time, perhaps years or even a decade, you may feel that there is a void in your life, however. This has been shown to occur in studies of very elderly people, who indicated that even though they were okay with their adjustment after the death of their spouse, they felt that there was still a void (Sable 1991).

You are reading this book probably because you feel a void and want to see what options you have to change your life, and so you may decide to try this process. To avoid feeling overwhelmed, don't look at the entire process facing you. Just take one moment and one day at a time. Make a plan for each day and set a very small goal. Remember, all of the tasks you have completed during your journey have had a purpose. The tasks will help you to reach this pinnacle in your growth process.

Your goal here is to recraft that piece of yourself that was defined by your late spouse or partner. Remember, this is a process. It involves tasting, sampling, and discarding on an internal, personal, substantive level, what does not feel good, comfortable, or congruent, and then integrating new ideas and images in your definition of your sense of self. This process differs from the surface change you achieved in the pseudoequilibrium stage. Think of it as a creative expression or an evolving work of art, such as a modern dance piece, except the product is you: a reshaped, reframed, and redefined you.

Even More Self-Reflection

During your change process you will learn about parts of you that you were never aware of before. One way to more easily see different parts of yourself is to choose an area of your life to develop and try new activities in that area. In trying and mastering new skills you will find that these small changes facilitate change in the overall character of your life. The exercise below gives you the opportunity to become aware of skills and talents you may have developed, and to look at areas of potential you may want to develop down the road. For example, Joann, a mathematician, had always wanted to take up the piano. Now that she was exploring new options, she decided to buy a piano and sign up for lessons.

1. First, pick three areas of focus for change, and write them here.

_____

_____

_____

2. Second, focus on how you will develop those areas of your life. Jot down some ideas.

_____

_____

_____

3. Prioritize your list from step one and pick one area to work on. Then begin.

As you begin to develop new aspects of yourself, you will find that you seek out others with similar interests and choose to be with those people. Moreover, as you meet and date new people, you will select those who are interested in the new, developing aspects of you. In that way, you will seek out people who may be different from those you sought out when you were married or shortly after your spouse died, reinforcing the new aspects of your evolving identity.

When you're working on these new skills, do not focus on the goal or end result. It's the process that's important. It will carry you forward to where you need to be. If you focus only on the goal, you may relinquish the flexibility you need to have in this stage so you can be open to new opportunities.

Not all women go through this internal growth process. As we discussed in chapter 4, some women in their seventies and eighties may prefer to seek the company of a male companion while continuing to use their late spouse as their frame of reference for decision making, and letting their adult children be their anchors in their day-to-day life.

DEVELOPMENTAL DIFFERENCES IN MEN AND WOMEN AT DIFFERENT STAGES

At this later stage of life you are facing different developmental tasks than you were when you met your first spouse. According to Gail Sheehy in her book *New Passages* (1995), women in their forties and fifties may be more aggressive than they were in their twenties and thirties, and older women in their fifties and sixties may start new careers after their children leave home.

Recently, while riding on a train I sat next to a woman who was widowed. After her husband's death, she had begun a new career for herself. Previously working as an art director, she now created her own art in her own studio, and displayed her work at galleries. She felt accomplished, satisfied, and pleased with this new career. She had a man in her life although she had not remarried.

In contrast, men in their forties and fifties begin to exhibit the feminine side of their personalities (Levinson 1986; Sheehy 1974). I have known men who in their younger years had very stressful, demanding careers that required them to be aggressive and then accepted less-stressful work later in life in order to reduce tension in their lives. Some men take up activities traditionally associated with women, like cooking.

For example, John worked for an advertising agency for years. At about age fifty-two, he decided to change his life and be less aggressive in his achievement goals. He became the head administrator of his church. He no longer had a long commute every day, he felt his work was more meaningful, and he was happier.

Clearly, if women become more aggressive and men become more mellow as they age, the basis for any new couple relationship is different from that of a younger couple. At this stage of your life you need to find a partner who is internally comfortable with himself or herself and is not threatened by you and the changes you are making in your new life as a single person.

The General Journey for Men

Men's adjustment process after the death of their spouse usually follows a pattern that is different from women's. Jack's story is a typical example of a man's adjustment experience.

Jack was devastated when his wife died of pancreatic cancer. He had been used to traveling overseas for business and letting his wife manage everything at home. Now he would have to take over managing the children, the family, the household chores—everything he never had to worry about before.

Jack was tearful, depressed, and lost. I referred him to a psychiatrist, who placed him on an SSRI, an antidepressant, which would allow him to concentrate. Several weeks later, I saw Jack again. With the help of his neighbors, he seemed to be getting some control of the household chores and his children. He had even started to develop a relationship with his daughter, with whom he had little connection prior to his wife's death.

Two months later, Jack was feeling jubilant and thought he might be ready to date. He started going on the Internet to meet women. He agreed to be careful, telling me that when he and his wife had met in college, they were very young, and sex was what they had in common—lots of it. But as they moved through life they had less and less in common. He had loved her dearly and had depended on her to manage the family and their home life, but this time around he wanted someone to be his companion. He looked forward to shared activities and shared moments together.

I never heard from Jack again. As with most men, after he connected with a new woman, he stopped therapy—a pattern noted by Dr. Morton Lieberman (1996) in his seven-year longitudinal study of widowed men and women. The implication is that the warm, intimate connection that comes with the therapy is met by the new woman and so the man no longer feels the need for therapy. Most men do not experience the intrapsychic emotional growth process after the death of a spouse. Instead, men may go through this growth process when they experience career changes or the loss of a job. But when it comes to relationships, men just tend to connect with a new woman and start a new life, allowing the woman to define their new social life.

So how useful is this book for men? The answer is very useful. Men typically like to avoid psychotherapy, preferring to do things for themselves. When lost they read a map to get directions. This book can be used as a road map by men who want to engineer their own change journey. Reading the chapters on the first, second, and third stages just as they are will benefit a man. While he may not need to experience internal personal change in order to move on with his life and so may not need to experience the transition to liftoff phase, a man can certainly benefit from reading about the experience of internal personal change and doing the exercises that go along with it. As a result, he will strengthen his sense of self and learn more about how women define themselves, which will make him a more understanding and reciprocating partner in a new relationship.

Men Who Experience the Internal Growth Process

Although most men do not undergo an internal growth process after their spouse dies, there are exceptions. Ronnie's experience is an example of such an exception. Ronnie's childhood experiences, his dysfunctional family history, and his individual personality made him vulnerable in his adult life. His poor sense of self and his inability to take charge of his own life made him a prime candidate for this dynamic personal growth process. Here is Ronnie's story.

Ronnie's wife, Elizabeth, died a painful death from cancer. Ronnie was devastated. He came to me saying that he needed to find out who he was or he would not survive. Ronnie was correct. Ronnie had depended on Elizabeth to run his life. Although controlling, she had been organized and supportive, and Ronnie needed someone like Elizabeth to be on top of him all the time. Now that his wife was dead, he needed to learn the skills that would allow him to take charge of his own life.

Ronnie stayed in therapy for years. Through the therapeutic process, he became aware of traumatic sexual and emotional abuse in his childhood. He had seen psychiatrists in his childhood, but they had labeled him the "crazy" one, the bad child in his family, which was actually dysfunctional.

Now, devastated by his wife's death and lack of structure and direction, Ronnie focused on learning about himself and crafting pieces of his identity so that he could function without his wife. Finally, at age seventy-one, Ronnie was about to make a major change and create a life for himself on his own.

Ronnie is a man who has to experience the recrafting process in order to get on with his life in a meaningful way. Some men like Ronnie, who are vulnerable because of early childhood trauma such as sexual abuse or other psychopathology, do not develop a strong identity and may be good candidates for the intrapersonal change process, which would allow them to successfully adapt to the death of their spouse.

A Special Situation

With some couples, after one partner dies, the other partner quickly becomes seriously ill or dies. This occurrence seems to support the theory that emotional loss causes enormous stress to the autoimmune system. Research suggests that closely connected couples may be intertwined emotionally and may not have their own strong independent identities (Zisook 1987). In these cases, psychotherapy, strong transitional anchors, and lots of support are important for the survivors to adapt to the loss of their spouses. Later, these people may benefit from parts of the change process to foster an independent ego (Levinson and Prigerson 2000).

Delores's Story

Delores experienced the intrapsychic change process several years after the death of her spouse. Delores's story is a model for those who choose to experience this part of the change process. Delores spent a year nurturing and caring for her ill husband. When he died she was exhausted. After her environment restabilized, Delores began going out with women friends. Eventually she was introduced to Brad, with whom she had a wonderful yearlong romance. After a while she found that what had begun as a nurturing involvement became boring and unfulfilling. Delores expanded her horizons and started reconnecting with old friends, taking classes, and involving herself in activities. Brad was upset and angry and tried to control her. So she ended the relationship.

Alone, sad, and in pain, Delores began to mourn the loss of this relationship. She was surprised at how much pain she felt. Was the pain only the result of her breakup with Brad? It could not be. In fact, she was finally experiencing sadness over her husband's death. She was at last able to begin to look at the loss and its meaning to her.

Slowly, day by day, Delores began examining her life. She listed the roles she had played during her marriage, and she assessed which roles were meaningful to her—she was a mother, a daughter, a friend, a professional. She looked at ways her husband was helpful in their relationship and not helpful. She thought about what she wanted now. Who was she? What did she like about herself? What did she want to change? What did she want to keep? Did she feel anchorless? Yes, in some ways. Yet in other ways she knew she had plenty of transitional supports.

Delores looked in the mirror. She took a good, hard look at what she saw. She knew she would have to make changes. She knew she would have to learn to be comfortable with herself alone, without a mate, before she would be ready to relate to a partner on a new and different emotional level of development. She needed to be anchorless for a time, but she could use transitional anchors to support her while she weathered the change process.

Delores's story is an example of how the change process works for women and how it may work for you. Your anchor is gone, and the roles he or she played in your life are gone. Some of the roles your partner played may be taken over by you. Others will just be left unattended. Other people may temporarily fill those roles for a period of time. In time you will learn to live with the discomfort caused by the void in your life and you will learn how to compensate. You may still feel a sense of loneliness or loss, but you will be able to function and manage.

As you see yourself changing, you will start to feel good about being able to accomplish tasks previously done by your spouse, or about successfully finding someone to help you with those things you can't do. You will have an exhilarating sense of accomplishment and empowerment as you watch yourself grow emotionally.

Remember, however, that this process is not easy. It is painful and difficult. You may find yourself crying or shouting in anger at your late spouse for dying and making your life so hard. That is okay. When you've calmed down, dry your eyes and do something nice for yourself until you are ready to push forward again. Go to a movie with a friend, take a weekend away, have a massage or a facial, or just spend an afternoon in bed with a good book.

Slowly, you will realize that you have moved forward and grown. Things that met your needs in the past may no longer meet your needs. Friends who were satisfying are no longer satisfying. Instead, you're finding other people and things to meet your needs—needs that have been recently defined in your new life without your spouse. What you are experiencing is intrapsychic change, emotional growth and maturation at a new and different level of development.

MOVING FORWARD

The internal growth process will help you reach a new level of emotional growth and development. Then you will be ready to craft a new chapter in your life and find a new level of contentment. The process will be difficult at first, just as it is when you begin any new and unfamiliar task. But in time you will adjust.

People who have experienced this growth process describe feeling like they are climbing out of a dark hole and up a flight of stairs where they see a light shining, drawing them upward. They feel that they are entering the world with new vision, new energy, new experiences, and much hope for a bright future. The new world appears full of possibilities and opportunities.

You are now ending the transition to liftoff phase of the journey. You are at a new level of emotional growth and development. You are now ready to integrate your new and changed self with a new environment. You are ready to enter the renewal and resolution stage of the journey.

Part III

Stage 3

Chapter 6

Renewal and Resolution

You have now completed three-quarters of your journey. You have just finished the dynamic phase of the personal growth process and are ready to meet the world again, only this time you are in a different place personally and emotionally. You have adapted to life in an environment without your late spouse. You have grown both internally and externally and you are ready to reexperience the world with new perspective. What pleases and satisfies you now is probably not the same as what pleased you during your marriage. Now you are going to look at the world with new vision. Thus, the world you integrate into your life will be new and different.

In time, you may meet someone you're interested in dating. This time, though, you will connect with potential mates on a new level of emotional growth, and the people you connect with will be at this same level of emotional growth.

A NEW CONNECTION

So you are now ready to date and connect with a new partner. In some ways, you are going back to the process described in chapter 4, but it will feel different because of the emotional growth you've done. You may be surprised to see how different you are in this new relationship from the way you were in your transitional relationship, and how different this connection is from your marriage.

You and your new companion may date for a while, and then you may begin to establish a relationship that will continue to evolve. The newness of the relationship is exciting, yet the developing rhythm of the new connection is calming and comforting.

You are beginning to experience a level of contentment you have only read about until now—you are internally peaceful.

A NEW AND BETTER RELATIONSHIP

To ensure that this relationship is a positive, constructive one, you may want to refer back to chapter 4 and the four factors that are required in order for a relationship to work (note that the second factor is now focused on integrating the children, rather than on their compatibility, as is appropriate at this stage): compatible baggage, ability to integrate all the children in the newly formed family, conflict resolution, and personal comfort.

As you progress in your new relationship, be aware of red flags that signal potential problems. Do not dismiss them and think they will either resolve themselves or just go away—they won't. Do not stay in a relationship that continues to have warning signs despite your attempts to resolve differences to your mutual satisfaction.

At some point you may be surprised at how easily this new relationship flows at the beginning and that it just gets better as time passes rather than becoming flawed. Remember the model of the seesaw, and think about this new relationship. How do you and your companion balance each other? Is one of you down when the other is up?

Lifestyle Issues

During the first part of the renewal and resolution stage you will focus on establishing a rhythm in your partnership. Then comes negotiating the lifestyle issues of the relationship.

You may want to answer the following questions:

1. Will you live together? _____

2. Will you merge finances? _____

3. Will you get married? _____

4. If you marry, will you have a prenuptial agreement? _____

5. How will you deal with living space? _____

6. Will you live in your partner's house or will he or she move to yours? _____

7. Or will you sell both houses and buy a new home together? _____

8. If you buy a new home, who will hold the title? _____

9. In the event that you or your partner dies, to whom will the house be left—to the other partner, to one of your estates, or to a child? _____

As you can see, you are now integrating your world with your partner's. According to Lowenstein and colleagues (1994), you can tell when you, a widowed person, are moving on with your life. The resulting lifestyle you establish is different from the life you had previously. Lowenstein describes the lifestyle as having a "new structure of meaning."

Finances

The question about how to negotiate finances with a new partner is complex. People in midlife come to a relationship with an established financial picture and lifestyle. And money may be a major issue for someone who's been widowed, since some of the assets and debts may be held in the name of the late spouse's estate or trust, making it even more complicated to merge one's finances with a new partner.

Another complication may arise when a woman is used to a certain lifestyle and discovers that as a widow she will no longer have the resources to support that lifestyle.

There is no simple formula for integrating two people's financial worlds. Each couple and each set of circumstances are unique. A few basic guidelines may help you determine how to approach the task of joining your finances.

First, keep in mind that money itself is usually not the only issue—it is a symbol, often of power, and it may be used as a basis for establishing power in a relationship. Prenuptial agreements are often valuable because they protect the asset base of both individuals, and they may limit the amount of tension among extended family members. Second, when negotiating finances in a new relationship, each person needs to be clear about what the other brings to the relationship and what monies are accessible to each partner. Third, it is important to clarify what steps, if any, each partner is going to take to protect the other in the case of one partner's death. Fourth, you'll need to address how joint properties acquired during the relationship will be distributed if one partner dies. The discussions about these issues, and the decisions you make together, further solidify the new partnership.

A simple example may help illustrate how financial issues can come into play in a new relationship. Newlyweds Jean and Joe had each lost a spouse and were coming to their new relationship with family money. They decided to live in Jean's house, sell Joe's house, and buy a vacation home together. They also decided that if something happened to Jean, Joe could continue to live in the main home for one year and would then find other housing. However, Joe would retain ownership of the vacation home until his death, at which point the vacation home would be sold and the assets would be split between the two surviving families. The same scenario would also apply to Jean if Joe were to die.

In another case, George and Miriam decided to sell each of their houses and buy a house together, the first joint project in their relationship.

One note of caution: It is important that you seek legal counsel when you make decisions related to property and money, since the laws of each state may dictate how you may proceed.

The Children

Two other major issues have to be addressed in order to successfully establish a meaningful life with your new mate. The first issue has to do with integrating your children into your life together.

In working with blended families, I frequently see people who have preconceived notions of the way families should work and attempt to impose these notions on their children. It is important to remember one thing: you and your children are a family, and your new mate is buying the whole package; however, your new mate is only *your* companion, not your children's stepfather or stepmother, until they welcome him or her into the fold. They do need to acknowledge him or her as your mate and give the respect appropriate for an older person, of course, but they do not need to accept him as Dad or her as Mom.

Most children, in time, are delighted to see their parent happy, since it lessens the pressure and burden on them. However, in cases where a man reconnects very soon after his wife dies, it is common for one or more of the children to be resistant to the new connection because he or she has not yet dealt with the other parent's death. Children process the loss of a parent differently than spouses, and time plays a big role. Children need a tincture of time to adjust to the loss of one parent before losing the other parent's emotional focus. Usually children are not able to deal with the loss of one parent until they are sure their surviving parent is okay, but they may be more tolerant of parents establishing their own lives a year or more after the other parent has died. Remember, change is difficult.

Thus, the couple needs to give the children time to adjust. During this period, the children should be given an opportunity to observe, meet, and join the blended family, but they should be allowed to stand on the sidelines for a while until they decide what they would like to do. They should not be forced to be part of the family until they are ready; however, they should not be allowed to disrupt the union or the family peace. Also, make sure each parent and his or her children have their own time together so that the children do not feel that they have lost their own parent and are now just part of a big group with no remaining connection to their old world. Remember, *you* have decided to connect with your partner; they have not. They are more likely to accommodate to your new world if you as their parent continue to give them a piece of yourself and a piece of their old world.

As you continue to work on the evolving relationship with your new partner, you have to consider how to integrate the children each of you have into your new family constellation. There are multiple factors which will influence this process.

The factors follows. Jot down the data from your newly blending family.

1. The age of the children: _____

_____

2. Their developmental stage in life (young, adolescent, married): _____

_____

3. Economic status if they are on their own: _____

_____

4. Congruence of life experiences, either negative or positive, both for the adults and for the children: _____

_____

5. Input from living ex-spouses who may be influencing the children: _____

_____

6. Role expectations and flexibility of all parties: _____

_____

7. Close relationships that existed prior to the new relationship: _____

_____

Let's look at each issue and explore its impact on the embryonic family system. The age and developmental stage of the children may be significant. If one of the partners has young children living at home, then the other partner has to be willing to accept the children as an integral part of day-to-day life. This is usually easier if it is the woman who has young children and the man's children are grown and more peripheral to your lives. If the man's young children are an integral part of your life, the situation becomes more difficult. The woman becomes a stepmother who is in charge of her own domain but has limited power over the children. In fact, in this situation it is essential that the father maintain supervisory charge of his children and create the structure and discipline, allowing the woman to play her appropriate role—as the husband's companion—not the role of substitute mother.

Developmental stages of the children should be considered. One developmental stage that may present difficulties is adolescence. Creating a new family carries with it plenty of stress. To add to this stress an adolescent who is acting out, doing such things as drinking and taking drugs, creates chaos and makes it almost impossible to integrate a newly merging family.

An adolescent who is using drugs and acting out may create irreparable difficulties in a newly blended family. It may be useful for a couple in this situation to continue the relationship but not merge households until the adolescent has left home, under either positive or negative circumstances, or has otherwise moved on and is no longer a part of the parent's daily life, particularly with regard to money.

A third dilemma is economic dependency of the children, whether young or grown. These needs should be discussed as you talk about living together. One woman, widowed three times, was in a fourth relationship with a lovely man. The problem was that he was financially enabling his alcoholic adult son. She did not have patience for this, so she went to visit her daughter in another city for the summer to give this man a chance to figure out what he was going to do with his son. She did not want to end the relationship, but she refused to take part in the enabling behavior. She was too old and too tired, and she just wanted a relationship that would give her peace at this stage in her life.

The children's similar life experiences and compatible socioeconomic backgrounds may be important in an integrated family. For example, if Julianne's children have all attended private schools and traveled throughout Europe while Greg's children have gone to public schools and only traveled to neighboring resort communities, family gatherings may prove to be difficult. Greg's children, who may not have had the broadening, life-enriching travel experiences that Julianne's children have had, may feel insecure and inadequate at joint family gatherings. In general, children from a middle-class background who have traveled widely even on a shoestring budget will fit more easily into shared family gatherings with children from a privileged background than would children with a more parochial upbringing. Children who do not feel comfortable may shy away from joint family gatherings, and their discomfort may put pressure on a newly formed couple relationship. Is there anything you can do to minimize the children's discomfort? Yes, there is. Consider holding low-key gatherings that may be comfortable for everyone involved, such as a picnic or other simple outing.

Input from other family members, such as ex-spouses, may negatively affect a newly formed family. For example, a close alliance between a mother and daughter may make the daughter hesitant to form a relationship with her father's new wife. The daughter may be afraid that her mother will be angry with her if she becomes a friend or even just an acquaintance of the new wife. So what do you do? Have patience. Allow the child to stay on the sidelines, and understand that the price she fears having to pay for joining the new family may seem too high for her at the beginning. As she grows and begins her own life and later her own family, she may become friendlier to her father's new wife, at least on a selective basis.

The issue of role expectations and flexibility of all parties is an important one. Imagine a woman who marries a widowed man hoping to meet her maternal needs by mothering his children. Or picture a divorced man, estranged from his children, who marries a woman with teenagers, wanting to become a father figure to his wife's children so that he can make up for the parenting he missed with his own children. In these examples, the woman and the divorced man may be greatly disappointed when the children do not accept them as a parent (they may be perfectly willing to accept their parent's new mate as simply a mate—just not as a parent). So what do you do when the children won't accept the new partner as a parental figure? Be grateful for small successes. Start small and be amenable to the terms requested by the children as long as they are not disrespectful or totally dismissive. An example of how this type of situation may manifest itself in real life is Marty's story.

Marty married Eleanor, whose sixteen-year-old daughter, Kim, lived with her. Marty knew Kim was a good child, but he liked everything to be neat and orderly, and so he often complained to Eleanor that Kim kept her books and clothes lying around and that she showed poor manners while eating. (In fact, Marty was letting Kim be the object of the same strict parenting he had had.) Eleanor was furious about Marty's complaints and asked him to look at Kim's positive qualities, instead of emphasizing her defects. In return Eleanor promised to work with Kim on keeping her belongings out of the communal family space. Eleanor told Kim that she could keep her room any way she wanted, and Marty conceded that the family room could also be untidy, but that the living room, kitchen, and dining room would need to be kept neat. Kim agreed to these terms. In this way, Kim, Marty, and Eleanor found ways to compromise and meet everyone's needs. As a result, the tension in the house diminished and Marty and Eleanor's relationship continued to develop.

The final factor that couples need to be aware of relates to integrating children into a newly forming family while reinforcing old alliances children have had with each parent prior to the new connections. It is important that you respect preexisting alliances and do not undermine them, which could mean disaster for your embryonic family. Understanding them and utilizing them, on the other hand, could enhance your new family structure. Diane's story is one example.

Diane and Jason had established a new family. Diane had a very close relationship with her daughter, Peggy, who often came home from college and expected that Diane would be available all the time. On one occasion when Peggy came home, Diane told her that she and Jason had a commitment and that she would not be available to Peggy that day. Peggy was furious. She sulked, staying in her room until she returned to college at the end of the weekend. Diane gave Peggy some time to calm down and then wrote her an e-mail message noting the inappropriate behavior and saying that they could have had a wonderful time together the second day Peggy was home, but that Peggy had been too busy sulking to enjoy any time with Diane.

On the one hand Diane was sad that her daughter's preexisting alliance with her ruined the visit; on the other hand Diane was glad that she had the opportunity to repair the damage before it had a more pervasive impact on the new family. Diane, aware that she would have to make an effort to reassure her daughter that she would always be there for her, decided she would go to Peggy's college town and spend a weekend with her. The plan worked. Peggy felt reassured that her relationship with her mother was still intact. On her next trip home Peggy was much more relaxed about her mother's relationship with Jason.

Alan is another example of a child who initially stays on the sidelines when the partners first come together, but later, when he is comfortable, connects in his own way to his parent's new companion. Alan had had a very close relationship with his father. After his father's death, Alan's mother, Dorothy, connected with Peter. Alan stayed on the sidelines and continued to rely on his other male support figures at the beginning of his mother's new relationship. But after a few years, Alan started seeking Peter out when his mother was not around. Alan would wait for him to come home from work late at night and then follow him around and talk to him about things that were going on in his life. Alan was transferring his connection with his father, probably unconsciously, to Peter. Peter never brought it up, but he enjoyed the moments with Alan as they presented themselves. He was pleased to be able to be a male role model to an adult male child. It met Peter's needs. This connection only happened because Peter and Dorothy were patient and did not demand anything from Alan. They just waited until he connected with Peter in his own way.

The above examples illustrate family dynamics and values being played out in new scenarios. These kinds of situations are stressful and certainly put a strain on the new couple relationship. Below are techniques that you can use to foster problem solving in difficult times:

1. Don't neglect the relationship between you and your partner and always be sure that you maintain the alliance between you. Remember to have regular dates with your new spouse. List three recent times that you and your new spouse have gone out on a date.

    _____

    _____

    _____

2. Keep the children's previous alliances in mind and acknowledge them. Think for a few moments. Who was each child closely connected to (for example, one parent, a sibling, or a grandparent)? Write down these alliances.

    _____

    _____

    _____

Make a plan to reassure the child that the connections are still there.

3. Identify the issue at hand that is important to the child and validate it (for example, college or a trip).

4. Search for alternative solutions that will reinforce the new couple relationship and still accommodate the child's needs in some way (for example, your child, who is away at college, needs some one-on-one attention, so you visit her by yourself for a weekend). Make some notes regarding possible solutions below.

    _____

    _____

    _____

These are important and difficult tasks. Some of these issues are illustrated in examples in the next three chapters, where you will see that finding solutions is often challenging.

One word of advice: You do not always need to be the solution finder. In some cases, presenting the dilemma to your children and allowing them to partake in solving the problem is itself empowering to them. You may find that they become willing participants who are very creative in presenting solutions. Moreover, they may be more willing to try new situations if they are the problem solvers and new ways are not imposed on them.

Integrating the children in the new relationship is one of the major tasks of a new partnership. One of the big mistakes couples make when trying to accomplish this task is to assume that in a new, blended family the hierarchy will follow the structure of a traditional family, namely the two parents on one level and the children on the next level. But the traditional family structure ends when the original family ends. The generational boundaries seem to change and it appears to work better if the couple's relationship can be solidified while the children have negotiating rights with the parents on a more equitable basis than in the traditional hierarchy.

Relegating Your Spouse's Memory to Your History

The second major issue of the renewal and resolution stage is relegating your late spouse's memory to your history. If you have come this far on your journey, then you have probably joined with a new, permanent partner and are creating a new chapter in your life. When you need to make a decision, you probably consult your new spouse and discuss how you might come to a decision together. You no longer conjure your late spouse to figure out what he or she would recommend.

This decision-making process is an example that you have moved on and carved a new structure of meaning in your life. But how did you get there and what becomes of the deceased spouse? Well, as you have read, carving a new structure of meaning is a process, and what happens to the deceased spouse is also a process. However, at the end of the process, it appears that the deceased spouse becomes a part of your history and a past chapter in your life. What role the deceased spouse plays in your current life depends on your new mate, your children, and the level of prominence you wish for his or her memory.

There are two basic options here. One, you may choose to never mention your late spouse, although this is not advisable. After all, he or she was the other parent of your children, and your spouse. Or two, you may mention him or her periodically, particularly at occasions such as graduations and weddings, and thereby honor his or her memory.

When Elaine's oldest son graduated from the same university her husband had attended, friends and relatives gathered to watch the son graduate. Later, at dinner, a toast was made to Elaine's late husband and to the university, and a toast was made to the new graduate. Elaine's new beau was at the event, only he very cleverly gave himself the role of taking pictures so that he would not intrude on a family event that had vestiges of Elaine's old life. So while Elaine was moving on with her new life, she was able to pause and salute her family's history and the memory of her late spouse.

Other situations have a similar flavor. Andrea's son was graduating from college. She invited her mother-in-law, her late husband's mother, to attend the graduation and made sure she would have a place of honor at the event. Several weeks later, Andrea threw an engagement party for herself and her new husband. She did not invite her mother-in-law to the engagement party, since it would not have been appropriate. Shortly thereafter, her son also got married, and of course Andrea included her mother-in-law in all the festivities surrounding her son's wedding.

Many years later, Andrea's mother-in-law died. She and her two sons went to the funeral, but she left her new spouse behind. It seemed fitting and proper that he not be a part of the funeral for her late husband's mother. After the funeral, Andrea, her children, and her late husband's extended family went back to the mother-in-law's house and spent an afternoon talking about the family, her life, and the end of an era. When Andrea and her two sons left her late mother-in-law's house, she knew that she was closing a chapter in her life.

When Polly's son was getting married, she invited to the wedding all the people who had been a part of her son's childhood. Many had been friends of her late husband. Although Polly's new companion was present at the wedding festivities, it was expected and appropriate that Polly's family friends toast her late husband and his memory at the event. In fact, several friends came specifically to represent Polly's late husband.

Every family has their own way of remembering a deceased spouse and parent. The ritual of memorializing the individual symbolizes the end of that chapter in the family's life and helps the survivors to move on to the next chapter in their lives. Some people do this by assembling photo albums, creating a specific memorial, or just putting aside time and talking about what they remember.

The renewal and resolution phase of your transition process is complete. You have successfully made an adjustment to the death of your spouse and have begun the next chapter in your life. Congratulations!

I have described the entire journey. Now I am going to tell you the complete stories of four people, Tina, Robert, Ruth, and Johanna, beginning with their spouse's illness or death and ending at the point where they considered their adjustment to be complete. By reading their journeys start to finish, you will be able to see how one stage evolves into the next part of the process. You may find these stories helpful to you as you craft your journey. You may find that you identify with some of the feelings, thoughts, or dilemmas these four people experienced. You may find their creative solutions to difficult problems helpful, or you may decide that you would have used a different solution to the problems they confronted as they began to adapt to the death of their spouse. At the end of each chapter, I pose a series of questions that will help you focus on important parts of each person's journey and how they might relate to your own journey.

Part IV

The Model in Practice

Chapter 7

A Young Widow's Story

Tina met her husband after college. They both were trail leaders and spent a lot of time together leading couples and groups on challenging trails in mountain ranges. They were used to handling problems and dilemmas posed by nature and were always managing risks that were presented by the trails.

Later in their twenties, they both trained for traditional professions. Soon, they married and began their life together, leading a traditional life in the suburbs, always reserving their vacations for revisiting nature, selecting a new mountain range and new trails each time. They again confronted risks and challenges as they scaled the steep mountains.

Back home, they began a family and had three children, a boy and two girls. Tina joined the PTA, took the children to Little League, ballet, and horseback riding lessons. Her husband coached the basketball team and led their son's Cub Scout troop.

THE TRAUMA

Then Tina's family life changed. At age forty-five, her husband was diagnosed with a terminal degenerative illness, and her life changed forever. All of the challenges she had handled on nature trails had not prepared her for what she now had to face. At age forty-two, Tina was going to lose her spouse—her friend, soul mate, and anchor.

Tina was scared, numb, and in shock. She knew she would have to raise her children alone, but right now she was busy managing the children and her house, and negotiating a maze of medical treatment and policies for which no amount of education could have prepared her. She did not have the time or energy to deal with her feelings. She just had to move forward minute by minute, day by day, taking care of the issue or crisis of the moment.

How did Tina feel? She did not know. She was functioning as an automaton. She was out of sync with her peers; she was living in the world of the sick and the dying while her friends were wrapped up in the world of the living. Mundane issues such as term papers, soccer games, and dinner plans for the weekend were her friends' priorities. Her priorities were her husband's medical procedures, blood tests, and various doctor appointments. Tina was the major emotional support person and central switchboard for her family. She had no time to rest and be replenished. She just had to keep going.

Periodically she would allow herself the luxury of breaking down and crying. Otherwise, just like on a mountain trail, she focused on the issue of the moment, namely her husband's needs, her children's needs, and her work. Days were too short. She never had enough time; there was always something else to do.

After a year, Tina's husband died. Tina went through the motions of greeting visitors and accepting condolences. A funeral took place, and lots of food was sent in. But all of this was a blur for Tina. She just had to get through it. Exactly what she had to get through she wasn't quite sure because she had no idea of what would come next. All she knew for sure was what had come before.

TINA WAS ALONE

Tina faced the reality of having three preadolescent children to raise, educate, and send off into the world. Yes, she had her career, medical insurance, and money to educate her children. And yes, her children would qualify for social security benefits. But money is not always the issue, although it does help to make life simpler and choices more varied, and having enough of it takes away the stress of making ends meet. Money would not serve as a substitute for her husband—the person she ran ideas by, the person who helped with the carpool, the person she wanted next to her as they watched their children grow, thrive, and begin to accomplish their goals. Their children were his legacy, and they were her legacy too. She knew she had to push forward so that their common goals regarding the children could be realized.

Alone at night, she became acutely aware of numerous mundane daily losses that do not become apparent until one loses a spouse. She realized that her husband would never walk in the door again at dinnertime. He would never share her bed again. He would never hold her hand again. They would never climb another mountain peak together again. He would not be there to share intimate moments or realize their dreams. Tina was alone and needed to begin to experience life alone.

After the funeral, all the people left. A few days later, good friends called and asked her to join them for dinner the following weekend. She accepted and then remembered that she would have to find a babysitter to stay with the children. While her husband was sick that last year, there had been little opportunity to go out, so hiring a babysitter had been the furthest thing from her mind. She decided to call the local college and see if they could recommend a student who could stay with the children. On the night of the dinner, she went out and met her friends. The dinner was pleasant, and she found it comforting to be out of the house in the company of friends. At the same time it was a shocking, glaring reminder that she was alone, no longer a part of a couple.

Tina's first trip to the grocery store was an eye-opener—she realized that she was shopping for four, not five. She no longer needed to think of her husband's favorite foods. What a profound way of confronting loss—seeing the food you no longer have to buy.

At home, Tina looked at her husband's side of the bureau in their bedroom and noticed all his things. He would no longer need his wallet. He would no longer need his credit card case, electronic organizer, or electric shaver. He was gone. Forever. And forever is a very long time.

Tina knew she could save the shaver and organizer for her children. But certainly by the time they would be old enough to use those items, technology would have changed and there would be new things on the market. New things in a new world that her husband would not be a part of. No, this is too overwhelming to deal with right now, she thought. She put these items away in a box to deal with at a later time.

TINA TREADING WATER

In the immediate days after the funeral was over, Tina walked around in a daze, feeling like she was in a dream (or nightmare), pinching herself to see if what she was experiencing was real. At other times she felt like she was having an out-of-body experience. This could not be real. She could not be experiencing all of this. Her life was not supposed to go this way. She should be cooking dinner for her husband and family, and then talking about their weekend plans.

All of a sudden Tina did a double take. She realized her husband would never sit at their dining room table again. They would never have him around to review their weekend plans. Tina started sobbing uncontrollably. Then she just stopped, dried her eyes, and went back to the activity she had so mindlessly begun.

Thus began Tina's adjustment process. She was beginning her journey one day at a time, one step at a time. Tomorrow she would get the children off to school. Then she had an appointment with the accountant. Later in the week, she had an appointment with her attorney. Each night she spent an hour writing acknowledgments to the people who had sent cards and gifts after her husband died.

Tired—yes, Tina was tired. However, nighttime was not Tina's friend. At night she was left alone with her thoughts, her anxieties, and her fears. Maybe one day she would have dreams again—new dreams, new beginnings. But right now she was left alone with herself, her husbandless self. Her doctor told her he would give her medicine to sleep if she wished. But Tina did not want to start using medicine just yet.

How were the children? They seemed sad. However, they were getting back into their routine fairly easily. The routine was comforting for the children. They had school, their friends, their activities. They did not have to focus on the vacuum in their home. They were busy. Tina would see how well they were doing at report card time, when their grades would indicate whether they were actually concentrating and studying effectively. In the meantime, the children's daily routine and her work kept her and them busy.

The need to manage her children's routines, settle her husband's affairs, and work at her job defined the first few months for Tina. Fortunately, there was no time for her to think, since she was not ready to confront herself.

The first few weeks and months flew by. Each day seemed to be endless but before Tina knew it, it was gone. Family and friends called, and people asked her to join them for social outings. Tina was not ready. Occasionally she would go to a friend's house for dinner, but more frequently she would have meals with her children and their friends and family after sporting activities. In some ways that seemed safer, more comfortable. She didn't have to see herself as husbandless and alone. She didn't have to see herself as the single person among many couples. So she sought shelter and comfort in child-focused activities.

PSEUDOEQUILIBRIUM BEGINS

Six months later, there seemed to be a routine, an order, to her life—by no means a desirable or complete routine, but nevertheless a routine and order. Tina received an invitation to a friend's special party at a dinner club. Tina decided that since it was an intimate gathering to mark a momentous occasion, she would go. She looked in her closet and realized she had nothing to wear. She did not like the way her hair and makeup looked. All of a sudden Tina was noticing herself and her image and she knew she wanted to make a change, but she did not even know what image she wanted to project.

At this point, Tina was about to enter the pseudoequilibrium stage of adjustment. It was as though she was about to go swimming and at first she would stick her feet in the water to test the temperature. She called one friend to get the name of a place to go clothes shopping, another friend to get the name of someone to do her hair, and a third friend to get the name of a place to get her makeup done.

She felt like she was reentering the world—the world of the living. It had been a long time. She was headed for an evening out. She felt a little strange, a little guilty—her husband would never get to go out again. How mundane to look at going out as important, she thought. But it was important. Tina was alive and she had to start living again—not just existing. So into the land of the living Tina would go. She did not need to feel guilty; she realized her husband would have wanted her to move forward and have a life. So she would make sure she dressed very carefully for the evening. She would have a good time for both of them—herself and her late husband. Yes, she would work to have fun.

The first outing was the most difficult. In time Tina found that she could go on these outings without guilt. In fact, she even learned to enjoy herself and not feel lonely. The next thing Tina had to face was making vacation plans for herself and her children for the summer. The family had always taken a weeklong vacation at the beach. Tina dreaded going to the same place they had always gone. All those memories—she would not be able to cope. What to do, where to go instead?

Tina gave it a lot of thought. She scouted the Internet for ideas, she chatted with the children and got their input, and she checked with friends to see what their plans were. After much consideration she decided she would look for a Sierra Club family trip. There were many choices. She checked with her children to see which adventure they wanted. They were hesitant but agreed to go after Tina conceded to taking the children on a shorter trip to the beach later in the summer. The children settled on a hiking trip in the High Sierras. Tina knew that Yosemite is a beautiful place and felt the structured adventure would be useful. She was pleased and relieved to have a compensatory plan to satisfy the children, who were used to taking a beach trip every year and needed consistency.

Even with the semblance of a routine that had developed, Tina's road was still bumpy. She was busy with the children and their activities, but she knew she needed to put some activities on the calendar for herself and for her own routine. She even found herself looking forward to doing this.

Tina looked to her girlfriends for support and for outings. Although most were married, they were supportive and connected to her, calling her regularly. Outings were scheduled around their own downtime, separate from their family activities. Tina did not mind. She valued the alone time. She knew she would have to find her own peer group but for now she was comfortable with the support she had.

Tina found that every attempt she made to do something new was an effort. Afterward, she felt exhausted. Tina noted how hard this adjustment process was. She found it much easier to just continue with her children and their issues. Her children's activities were known territories, but her new social life was not. There were times when Tina just wanted to curl up in a ball and hide in her room, and sometimes she did. Other times she was courageous and felt okay with what new adventures she undertook.

During the first year after her husband died, Tina found each holiday to be very painful. All the old memories of holidays past emerged. She was sad and uncomfortable. Tina kept asking herself how she would ever get through this. She did not know how, but she knew she would. The first year finally ended.

When she faced the second year, Tina was comforted by the thought that she had already experienced each holiday once. In some way it had to be easier, and she knew that she had negotiated one big hurdle—the first year. This second year, one of her children would finish middle school, and she would have to experience a graduation alone. She dreaded the event, but for now she would put it on the back burner and move forward.

The one-year anniversary of her husband's death was marked with a little ceremony. Then she gathered her children and brought them into the family den. She started talking about her husband and told a story about something he had done. She encouraged each of the children to tell a story they remembered about their father. They laughed and cried together. Tina decided they would mark the anniversary this way every year. The children agreed that it was a nice way to remember their daddy.

Days rolled into weeks. Weeks rolled into months. Time just continued to march on. The quality of Tina's life remained the same. She went to dinners with friends, she worked, she took care of the children. But she also began to expand her social horizons to include single friends. She started by making one social engagement every other week, sometimes to the theater, sometimes to the symphony.

Tina knew she could go to a support group. However, she nixed that idea. She did not want to go somewhere to listen to stories of sadness and woe. She had been dealing with illness, grief, and sadness for more than two years. She wanted a vision of light and brightness and joy. She had enough trouble with her own pain. She did not want to spend her limited personal time listening to others' painful tales. She had been among the sick and dying for a long time. She now wanted to be among the living and move on with her life.

TINA AND DATING

About two and a half years into the adjustment process, Tina had lunch with a good friend. Tina noticed on the way to lunch that there was a spring in her step. She noticed that she was smiling more. As long as she did not look too far into the future she was okay. So she started to review her life and where she was at the moment.

Tina was working and busy with the children's activities, but she did not have a social life as a single person. Her friend asked how she felt about dating. Tina did not know what she thought or felt about dating at that moment, so she reflected. She realized that she would be so vulnerable. She had hated the dating scene when she was a young adult. To face the dating scene again now was more than she could handle. On the other hand, she did not want to remain a widow for the rest of her life. She knew she would have to confront the issue at some time. But she was not ready to confront it now.

Her friend was kind and compassionate. She reassured Tina that she understood her situation. Tina thought, "Of course she can be sympathetic, but she cannot understand my situation, because she is not widowed." This friend had not experienced what Tina had lived through. She did not have to deal with a husband dying. She did not lose her best friend, her soul mate, her anchor. She did not have to live with the thought that she was the sole parent left to raise her children. She did not have to start her life all over again.

Tina was surprised at her strong reaction. She did not realize how angry she was. Why was she lashing out at her friend? She did not need to. She felt bad about lashing out, but her friend did not have to change her life and Tina did. Fortunately, her friend was a safe person for Tina to talk to. She would not lash back at Tina or make judgmental comments about Tina's inaction. Suddenly Tina felt exhausted just thinking about all the changes she still had to go through, so she decided to put it all aside for the time being and go home and take a nap.

The lunch date Tina had with her friend was a crossroads in her life. Tina realized that she would have to reach out and find some single friends who would understand what she was facing. They also might be able to give her some dating tips. Tina decided to create a list of friends whom she might contact.

Then Tina remembered Marian, a woman with whom she had gone to college, whose husband had died six months before Tina's, and thought perhaps she would be willing to reconnect. She decided to call her. Marian was surprised and delighted to hear from Tina, and she happily agreed to introduce Tina to some of her single friends.

Several months later, Tina was out with some new acquaintances, and during the evening a woman asked whether Tina would be receptive to a date, saying she had the name of a man who had recently been divorced. He was nice, had custody of his children, and was looking to meet women to date. Tina was stunned. All of a sudden she had to think of herself as a sexual being. She responded by saying she would be delighted. But internally she was asking herself whether she would really be delighted. She did not know the answer to that question.

Several days later, the man, Eric, called and asked Tina for a date for that Thursday evening. They would have dinner and get to meet each other. What to wear? Tina was frantic—she was not sure what image she wanted to project. She decided on casual. She would project an understated image and be low-key. She did not want to give any wrong indications.

A date! She had not dated since her twenties. What would it feel like? She was nervous and anxious. She had butterflies in her stomach. Would he like her? Why did she care? Would she like him? What was the dating protocol today? Who would pay for dinner? Should she offer to pay her share or should she assume that he would pay?

Fortunately that week passed quickly. Tina found a babysitter. She wondered what she would tell her children about where she was going. She decided to be truthful with them and tell them she had a date. The children appeared annoyed when she told them. They seemed indifferent and defensive. Tina tried to reassure them that this man was just company for her, that she was not looking to replace their dad.

Tina decided to meet the man in a public, neutral, and conveniently located place, but one located in a neighborhood away from where she lived, so she wouldn't run into very many people she knew. She did not want him to come to her house the first time. She especially did not want to introduce her children to multiple men if she ended up dating a lot, particularly at the beginning. Her plan was to meet the man, spend two hours having dinner, and be back in time to tuck the children into bed.

She met Eric at the appointed restaurant, an interesting place, quiet, softly lit, with simple food. Upon meeting him, Tina was surprised. He was a pleasant-looking man, appearing older than she had anticipated. As they greeted each other and talked—basically interviewing each other—Tina noticed that the awkwardness of the moment began to disappear.

At the same time, she could not believe she was out on a date. A date. That felt strange. She remembered dating when she was twenty-something, and here she was again. She had never expected that to occur.

Tina observed Eric carefully. He was of medium height, well built, and not heavy. He was pleasant in his manner, and slightly nervous. Eric started by telling Tina about his work and then about his children. He had two daughters, both adolescents, both good students. Eric was involved with the girls and their sports programs.

After Tina told Eric about her family, the two talked about interests they had, looking for areas they had in common. The evening hours passed quickly and pleasantly. A friend had suggested that she end the date while they were still going strong, so she did. Eric asked her whether she would like to see him again, and she nodded yes. Eric said he would call.

Tina got in her car and let out a big sigh of relief. She had just surmounted a big hurdle. Now she could go home to her safe harbor, tuck her children into bed, and later, and when it was quiet, process the event. When she got home she did not discuss the date with her children, only briefly answering questions they asked her.

In the middle of the following week, Eric called and asked Tina for a second date for the coming weekend. Tina agreed. They would go to the movies and have a late-night snack. She told the children she was going out again. Again they seemed disinterested and slightly annoyed. Clearly, the children were taking a defensive posture and did not want to be involved with their mother's social life. Tina noted but did not respond to the children's behavior, and she proceeded with her plans.

A RELATIONSHIP BEGINS

Tina continued dating Eric for several months until she hit a crossroads—it was time to decide whether they should become sexually intimate with each other. According to her friends, she was lucky that he had not put pressure on her to go to bed with him; they had told her that you have three safe dates, and then the man wants to have sex.

Tina did not know whether she was ready to cross the line and become sexually intimate with anyone. It had nothing to do with Eric; he was nice enough. Rather, it had to do with whether she was emotionally ready to leave her husband's domain and cross into the domain of another man.

Tina processed the issue. She had needs, but she was getting some of her physical needs for human touch met by having facials and massages. Tina thought, How do you know that you like someone enough to go to bed with them? Did she want to spend the rest of her life with Eric? Probably not. But did she need to spend the rest of her life with a man in order to allow herself to have sex with him? She kept asking herself that question, and she finally arrived at the answer: probably not. She did not need to be focused on the long term; she just needed to move forward. What she probably needed to do was think about being intimate. Did she want to be intimate? She decided to give it a try.

Sex. Where would they have it? Certainly not at her house, not in the bed she shared with her husband—a friend had warned her about that—although she knew that at some point she would have to buy a new bed of her own. Eric suggested going to his place. His daughters wouldn't be there, and they would have privacy. He said he would be happy to take Tina there, but only if she was comfortable; otherwise they could go to a hotel. Tina was sure she did not want to go to a hotel.

So Tina and Eric became intimate. The first sexual encounter was somewhat surreal for Tina, but she persevered. She found that the second and third sexual encounters were easier as she became more comfortable with her nudity, her body, and Eric's body. Tina and Eric's relationship moved forward. Now Tina had her work, her children, her extended family, and Eric, although she did not know what to call him at this time. More than a date, but not her permanent partner, he was her "for now" companion.

Eric and Tina continued this way for six months, and then she decided to introduce him to her children. They all went ice-skating together. The activity gave the whole group a common thread and diluted the intensity of the meeting. Furthermore it allowed Tina's children to get to know Eric a little better, and it would give Eric an opportunity to learn about Tina's children. The event went well, but having an "everyone together" activity was not something that Tina wanted to do again soon. She found herself feeling anxious, fragmented, and worried about how everyone was doing. In time, she thought, if the relationship moved forward, she would do this kind of activity again, but for now she would keep her relationship with Eric separate from her interactions with her children.

Then Eric introduced Tina to his children, and that meeting seemed easier to Tina. The children were receptive and the event went smoothly.

As Eric and Tina's dating continued, they developed a routine. Periodically they experienced some conflict, but to Tina's surprise, they seemed to be able to resolve the differences fairly easily. She had heard all sorts of horror stories about conflicts in new relationships, which had worried her. But she did not have difficulty negotiating speed bumps with Eric.

When they had been dating about a year, though, Tina began to notice a series of new behaviors. Eric was acting differently than he had at the beginning. He was becoming comfortable with his and Tina's relationship and not going out of his way to make an effort. Sometimes he would cancel a date at the last minute, and he called her less frequently.

Tina noticed that their fun, easy relationship was becoming work. She noticed that she was less happy and less satisfied than she had been before. She had a talk with Eric, but he denied the behaviors she confronted him about. Tina felt frustrated. Tina decided to end the relationship. She told Eric that she needed a break and asked him not to call her for two months.

THE INTERNAL GROWTH PROCESS

Tina felt relieved after ending her relationship with Eric. She did not need someone else's baggage to complicate her life—she had enough of her own. But she also noticed that while she was relieved to be rid of Eric, she was experiencing a pervasive sense of deep sadness. The sadness persisted. Tina had not felt the need for a therapist up to now, but now she was ready. She asked around for the names of a few good therapists and called for an appointment.

Hearing Tina's story, the therapist confirmed that her feelings were normal. Having gained a little distance and perspective, she was now ready to process the death of her husband differently than she had processed it before. Tina left the therapist's office feeling introspective. She would do some thinking as soon as she cleared her calendar and was able to get some time and space. Over time, Tina began to process the death of her husband. The therapist had given Tina some tasks and she could now focus on that work. She began to sift and sort what had been good and meaningful about her marriage, and what had been missing in it. Next she looked at her relationship with Eric—a relationship forged at the wrong time by two people who were needy, lonely, and vulnerable. No wonder it fell apart. It did not have the solid ingredients it would have needed in order to continue.

Then Tina took a deep breath and stood in front of the full-length dressing mirror in her bedroom. She looked long and hard at what she saw. Here was a middle-aged woman looking slightly worn and more wrinkled than others in her age group. She had been through a life experience usually reserved for older people, and she was saddened and worn out by her experience.

Who was she? What did she want to be? What did she do well? What was she not good at? What did she want her new life to consist of? Did she know? Did she dare allow herself the time and opportunity to think about the future? Or the past?

Tina withdrew from her social activities for a few months. She decided she needed a period of time when she could be introspective. She reviewed the different periods in her life and examined her strengths and weaknesses. She focused on her vulnerabilities. What would make her feel more comfortable with herself? How could she compensate for her sense of inadequacy?

She realized that she had counted on her husband for his financial strengths. Now that he was gone, she needed to know that she would be okay on her own for the rest of her life. She needed to know that she could build her own reserves financially and be capable of managing her own money. How would she go about doing it? She spoke to her accountant and asked him what he suggested. He recommended that she attend some money-management seminars and read some educational materials. She resolved to try one financial seminar and begin to learn, even though it might take a long time. She wanted to know that if she connected with a new man it would not be so that she'd have someone to manage her financial affairs for her. It was about more than not depending on a man. It was about feeling competent in an area she had not felt competent in before. It was about feeling a sense of accomplishment—that she could take care of herself.

At this point Tina was not ready to go out on another date, but she was feeling better about herself. She was ready to go out again with her women friends and face the world with a new outlook. Tina knew that she was now more self-confident and that she was in a different place. After a few months she was ready to meet another man and begin anew.

RENEWAL AROUND THE CORNER

Tina met and dated two different men, but they weren't her cup of tea. Then she met a third man who was different from anyone Tina had known, and she went out with him. Much to her delight, Tina found this new man interesting and engaging. As time went by, she continued to see him, but she proceeded very slowly. Their outings were always fun. Conflicts arose but were quickly resolved. She developed a routine with this new man.

As she got to know him better, she wondered whether their respective baggage was compatible. She went through the list of factors to consider, and all were workable. Her children were ready to meet him. She was ready to meet his children.

In time, Tina found that she and her new mate had integrated their lives. She was pleased with his company, pleased with how he interacted with her children, and comfortable with their life together. Her life was truly taking on a new character, different from her old life. Although all of her children were not thrilled, they accommodated the new man in Tina's life. She gave her children time to accept him.

It had now been four years since her husband's death. Her new companion was in her life to stay. So she felt she needed to memorialize her husband so she could allow him to be a part of her past, not her present. Tina needed to give it some thought. She decided that she would put together a list of options, such as a donation to an environmental group, a plaque at a mountain cabin or national park, or a donation to fund the repair of a favorite mountain trail, and then she and her children would make a decision.

Tina knew that she still had a lot of work to do, but she was not concerned. She decided to take one day at a time. She knew she was in a different place than she had been before. She knew that the life she and her new mate would carve out would be different from the life she had lived with her spouse, and that their lifestyle would evolve in time. Tina knew that she was beginning the next chapter in her life.

QUESTIONS ABOUT TINA'S ADJUSTMENT

1. What aspects of Tina's story do you identify with, if any?

_____

_____

_____

_____

2. Identify the three stages of her adjustment journey.

_____

_____

_____

_____

3. Are there aspects of Tina's journey that you have difficulty with? If so, why?

_____

_____

_____

_____

4. Are there ways that you feel Tina could have avoided difficulties in her journey?

_____

_____

_____

_____

5. If you were Tina, would you handle these difficulties in the same way that she did? In a different way? How?

_____

_____

_____

_____

Chapter 8

A Widower's Tale

Robert's wife died after a bout with cancer that lasted three years. He knew she was lucky to have those three years of time, although her quality of life in the last year was not wonderful. Robert and his wife made the best of the few special moments they had during those last few years.

Now that she was gone, Robert felt alone and lost. He was in his midfifties. He had his work, and his children were beginning their careers. He did not know where to turn. How would he move forward?

Robert's first major adjustment had come when his wife had stopped work two years ago. Although she had had a disability policy, it did not cover the daily living expenses she had assumed responsibility for while she was working. It had been an adjustment to cover the extra expenses, but Robert and his wife had managed, and he felt good about that. Now he had to adjust his lifestyle again so that he could live on one salary and pay off the huge amount of medical bills incurred during his wife's illness. Fortunately his children, a son and daughter, were now self-sufficient, so he didn't have to worry about supporting them.

Robert had a son, Jonas, and a daughter, Samantha, who lived in different and distant cities. Jonas, a lawyer, worked long hours in a large law firm in New York. Samantha was living in San Francisco and carving out a life there. Robert was at home alone and faced building a new life for himself.

At the beginning of his adjustment, Robert made very simple and concrete decisions about his daily activities. What should he fix for dinner tonight? Before his wife got sick, Robert had cooked minimally. It became a necessity that he learn to cook good, nutritious meals after his wife became sick. Robert took a series of cooking classes and read cookbooks. He found that learning different cooking styles helped him to not focus on the enormity and severity of his wife's illness. It was much easier to focus on different kinds of pasta than on her impending death. In the process, Robert found that he actually liked to cook. Now, he thought that perhaps he would expand his cooking skills and work on different dishes.

STARTING OVER

The funeral was over. His children left to go back to their lives. Paperwork needed to be done. Acknowledgments of condolences needed to be written. Everything his wife used to take care of was now on his shoulders. He was overwhelmed. He felt not lonely, but very alone.

Where should he begin? He did not even know. When his wife's best friend called and offered to have him over for dinner that Sunday evening, he was very happy to accept. What a welcome refuge. Then she offered to come over on Monday and help him get started writing acknowledgments to people who had sent condolences.

At first it was hard for Robert to let down his guard with her and admit how he felt. However, his wife's illness taught him that embarrassment was a useless emotion in times like this. It seemed that he could not avoid letting *someone* know how vulnerable he was. So why not his wife's best friend? She had been there through thick and thin; she had helped his wife deal with each negative medical report and later helped her face death. Certainly she could help him face life.

Was he being disloyal to his wife? No—he knew his wife would have wanted him to ask Alice for help so that he would not have to feel so isolated and alone and flounder so badly. She would have wanted Robert to be comforted. She had trusted Alice with her life, and she would trust Alice to steer Robert correctly. Robert concluded that he did not have to feel guilty about asking her.

Alice was happily married, so she was not looking for Robert to connect with her. She was just being kind, but he wondered what friends would think. Will they gossip? Robert realized that he could not worry about what others would think or say. He would have to move on with his life and do what was right for him.

Robert went to Alice's house for dinner on Sunday night. Pot roast and potatoes had never tasted so good. The warmth of the house and the inviting welcome he received made him feel very comfortable and safe. He knew that this was what he needed, and he let down his guard. Alice's husband, Paul, was kind and welcoming, gently clapping Robert on the back and saying that he hoped Robert was doing okay. Of course, Robert nodded in the affirmative. Paul did not have a clue about how hard it was.

The evening went by quickly. Robert did not want to leave the warmth and comfort of their home and their friendship, but he did not want to overstay his welcome and left at eleven o'clock. Alice told him she would be at his home by ten the next morning. Robert felt the need to reassure Paul that all they would do was to write acknowledgments, and Paul nodded his understanding. The evening at Alice and

Paul's was a good icebreaker for Robert. He knew he could take the difficult first steps the next day and move forward.

Alice came the next day. They spent two hours writing acknowledgments and then Alice excused herself to run errands. Having the help getting started made all the difference in the world. Robert knew he would be able to complete the rest of the cards himself now.

Robert packed up the cards and went to a nearby indoor golf facility to hit balls. With each ball he hit he could feel the tension leaving his body. When he returned home later that afternoon, he got in the shower and for the first time in weeks gave himself permission to let go. He sobbed.

Out of the shower, he regained his composure and got dressed. He looked at the movie listings in the paper, selected a good war flick, and marched himself off to the movies. He could have gone to the video store and brought home a movie, but he thought it better to go to a theater. Coming home later, he could make himself a light dinner and go to sleep for the night. Yes, that was a better plan.

Robert found that the dinner at Alice's was a good beginning. Other friends called him to have dinner at their houses, and his children kept in touch. He was able to move on with his transition journey.

Days ran into weeks. The house was empty, and he missed his wife—her smile, her smell, her kind words when he walked in at night. Robert found that he was able to manage as long as he focused on the immediate day, the immediate week, and the immediate moment. He did not look into the future. It was all he could do to cope with being in the present. He would deal with the future later.

Robert's children both invited him to come visit, and so he decided to spend a long weekend with his son in New York, and later a whole week with his daughter in San Francisco. He found having the trips scheduled provided him with structure and a diversion to look forward to.

In New York he would visit galleries, go to shows, and have some nice meals. In San Francisco, he and his daughter would spend the weekend in the Napa Valley, stay in a bed-and-breakfast, and visit wineries, bike through the valley, and maybe indulge in a mud bath. These would not be painful trips to make because they were not places he had been with his wife. Moreover, he needed to solidify his individual relationship with each child now that his wife was gone. Having this as a focus helped to decrease the sense of purposelessness he had been feeling since his wife died.

Yes, his work continued. But work is work. Robert liked his work, but since his wife became ill, he had become acutely aware of what is really important in life: people, relationships, taking time to smell the roses, and just taking time to do those things that are important to you.

Robert thought for a moment. What regrets did he have about his wife? He regretted that he had not told her enough over the years how much he loved her. He regretted they had not taken enough vacation time and spent time together exploring new areas. He regretted they would not walk their daughter down the aisle together. He regretted . . .

Robert stopped. That was enough time spent on self-pity, he decided. Instead, he would focus on cooking, an activity that he enjoyed, so he could stop dwelling on his feelings. He would buy himself a new cookbook, and he would find a cooking school and attend a weekend cooking class. Robert felt better.

Robert found that the trips to New York and San Francisco were very refreshing. Spending time with each adult child alone allowed him to initiate a new relationship with them, his own relationship, a relationship in which he could discover their strengths as individuals and they could learn about him as a person, not just as their father.

On the New York trip Robert was surprised to see how receptive and responsive Jonas was to his vulnerabilities and needs. Jonas had planned the whole weekend. He took Robert to galleries, selected plays for them to see, and made reservations at carefully chosen restaurants—establishments that highlighted food styles that were his specialties.

Robert was able to learn about his son in ways that he would not have if his wife had been present. Robert was sad that it took his wife dying for him to add this new dimension to his life. Nevertheless, he and Jonas would now have their own relationship. Did Robert feel guilty? Ever so slightly. But he was pleased that there was so much the two of them had to work on together, and he looked forward to more visits with his son. It was a whole new scenario.

His trip to San Francisco also proved productive. His daughter, Samantha, was more laid-back about making plans than his son had been. Robert could see that her relaxed personality was well suited to life on the West Coast. She seemed happy with her work, her life, and her activities. She took Robert to the San Francisco Museum of Modern Art, the Yerba Buena Center to see a Smuin Ballet performance, and the opera. Robert could not believe that he had agreed to go to the ballet; taking their daughter to the ballet had always been his wife's role. Much to his surprise, Robert found that he liked the performance. It was quite an experience for him, and in fact he found himself looking forward to going again.

On the weekend Robert and Samantha drove to the Napa Valley. They roamed the streets of Calistoga, visited a winery or two, and had dinner at the Culinary Institute of America, which she had chosen because she knew he liked to cook. They stayed at a warm and intimate bed-and-breakfast nearby, and Robert was surprised at how satisfying the accommodations were. The bed-and-breakfast would never have been his choice if his wife were along; he only stayed in chain hotels or resorts. How ridiculous his priorities had been, he realized. He must remember to keep an open mind to new ideas now. After all, his old life was over. He now had to create a new and satisfying life for himself.

The trip was a success. He had learned new things about his daughter, and he also had an opportunity to see pieces of himself in her that he would have never recognized in the past.

Robert went home from his trip feeling that he was now in a different place. Whereas before he had been somewhat removed from his children's lives, now he was intimately involved with them as individuals. This was a door that he never would allow to close again.

The next few weeks and months flew by. Robert worked during the week. Occasionally, he would call friends and invite himself for dinner, but mostly he looked forward to following the new routine he had established for himself. After work he went to the gym and worked out. Then he went home and began work on a recipe he had selected over his morning coffee. If he needed additional ingredients, he would pick them up on his way home from the gym. Focus on the recipe made the time fly by, and he was pleased to be able to handle the evening by himself.

On weekends, he would join one of the five couples in his social group for dinner. He just rotated from one couple to another each weekend, and fortunately they were lovely about including Robert in their social world.

Eight months after his wife had died, Robert was having lunch with a good friend after a round of golf. His friend looked at Robert and asked what his plans were. Robert asked him what he meant. The friend continued, "It will be the one-year anniversary of your wife's death in a few months. What will you do to mark the occasion? After the anniversary, will you consider dating?" Dating? Robert thought, feeling stunned. He had been so focused on the here and now that he had not thought about the future, and he had specifically avoided thinking about dating. The friend asked Robert if he would join him and his wife on a trek to Machu Picchu, or perhaps a rafting trip down the Colorado River. The trip part sounded great, but the dating part he had to put aside for a while.

Robert knew he missed female companionship, but couldn't he just skip over the dating part, he wondered, and have a female friend? Dating scared him—he did not want to be on display. However, Robert knew it would be okay with his wife if he dated. They had talked about it before she died, and she had said she did not want him to be alone.

Thinking about it further, Robert was glad that his friend had brought up the subject of dating and made him confront what he was avoiding. However, Robert was more at ease with the trip idea and decided to work on the trip plan with his friend, and maybe confront the dating issue after the trip. A much better idea, he thought. Take one hurdle at a time!

The first anniversary of Robert's wife's death came. Robert and his children went to the cemetery to visit his late wife's grave, and they spent a quiet weekend together, which flew by for Robert. It was a warm, intimate experience for him to spend time with his children both individually and together. They talked about their mother and the things about her that they missed, about her illness and how hard it was to see her suffer and fail, and about watching their mother die and how it had affected their individual lives. They realized that the experience taught them how precious and short life is. They learned to appreciate life and nature—flowers, vegetation, and the seasons. They know that there is more to life than football scores.

The children also talked about the intimate time they were having with Robert and how new it was for them to learn about this side of him. While their mother was alive, he was more distant to them, and they were looking forward to getting to know him better as an individual. His daughter asked for a piece of her mother's jewelry so she would have something special of her mother's to keep with her. Robert was touched and made sure he put aside time to go over her mother's jewelry with her.

The children asked Robert what his plans were. Did he plan to sell the house? Did he plan to travel? Was he going to continue working or was he looking forward to cutting back? (Both the children and Robert avoided the obvious question: Was Robert going to date?)

Robert was still just taking one day at a time and didn't have any big plans. He knew he would continue working, since work was comfortable and gave him structure for his day. And he would plan a trip to visit each child so that he would have something to look forward to down the road. But he knew that he had to do something else. He would talk to his friends to get ideas.

Shortly after his children left, his wife's good friend, Alice, called. She asked Robert whether he would consider going on a date. She told him that many of her friends had been calling her and asking whether Robert was ready to date. Robert hesitated, so she made a suggestion. She told Robert that she had a particular woman in mind, and she described the woman to him—divorced, a few years younger than him, and attractive. She then suggested that Robert call her and ask her to have coffee with him.

Much to his surprise, Robert felt okay with that plan. The structure gave him a sense of support. It made him feel more comfortable and less anxious about taking this next step in his adjustment journey. He was glad about Alice's call and was surprised to find that he was not as scared to call the woman now that he had some direction.

That afternoon he called the woman, Jan. He introduced himself, told her how he had gotten her name, and asked if she would like to meet for coffee, and she accepted. The plan was to go to a new café in the area and have dessert and coffee. He was also advised to time limit the meeting so that they both would enjoy a second meeting. Although Robert had butterflies in his stomach, he also looked forward to the idea of having company.

The day of the coffee date came. Robert picked Jan up at her home. (Since they both had friends in common, she was comfortable having him meet her on her home turf instead of in neutral territory.) He noticed that she was pleasant looking, in fact quite pretty, and very welcoming.

They went for coffee and spent two hours learning about each other and their stories. Then Robert (acting on the advice of friends, who had recommended limiting the time of the date even if it was going well) said that he had a business appointment to get to and would need to end the date, but he asked if she would be willing to see him again. She answered yes. Robert felt like a little boy. He was excited and relieved that she had not rejected him. He felt old yet he felt young. It was an unusual feeling—he had been here before, yet he was starting all over.

Robert called his wife's friend and thanked her. He said little about the meeting except that he had had a pleasant meeting with Jan and, yes, they would be seeing each other again. His wife's friend suggested that they all go to a concert together the following week and have a bite to eat afterward. Robert agreed and hung up the phone, and then he stopped for a moment and thought about steps he had just taken. He knew he was entering the world of dating, whatever that world held for him.

Robert called Jan and told her about the plan to go to a concert and invited her to go. She accepted, and so began Robert's first dating experience.

Over the next few months Robert continued seeing Jan. They went to movies, art galleries, and concerts. They had dinner with friends and dinner by themselves at their homes. Robert even ventured to share his good cooking with her, and Jan was a delighted recipient.

Soon Robert felt that it was time to cross the next hurdle, and he approached Jan about becoming intimate. She did not hesitate. She had been divorced for five years and was at peace with her divorce, and Robert was not the first man she had dated since her divorce, so she too was ready for intimacy.

Becoming sexually intimate with Jan was easier and less awkward than Robert had imagined. He was surprised at how good it felt to touch another human being and how much he had missed being touched in return. It felt good to physically connect.

After the first physical encounter, Robert asked himself if he felt guilty, and the answer was no. He knew that he had waited long enough to have sex, and his wife would have wanted him to make a new life for himself—she had given him permission. Surprisingly, he felt sad, deeply sad. He realized that his life with his late wife was truly over, and the sadness was a reflection of his mourning the end of their emotional connection.

After a few days Robert felt better. The sadness went away. He called Jan, made plans for the weekend, and focused on the next challenge—when and how would he tell his children about his relationship with Jan.

In the meantime, Robert and Jan explored each other's lives, they explored each other's bodies, and they talked about each other's children. Both were careful not to talk about a future; rather, they just stayed in the here and now. Yet both of them knew that they had to address the future at some point.

They did have some conflict. Jan began to assert herself in ways that were new to Robert. Robert was surprised at first. Then he learned to step back and think about how to respond. What was important to him? In what circumstances could he comfortably give Jan her way without giving up a piece of himself? The first conflict was the most difficult—it took a week for Jan and him to have their first official fight and find a resolution to it. Thereafter the fighting was easier—the resolutions came more quickly. However, Robert found ways to be very clear and definitive about the areas where he would not compromise.

As time continued it became apparent that Jan and Robert were integrating their lives together. But they still had to deal with the children. Robert felt that telling his son would be easy. He was more concerned about his daughter's reaction, guessing that he would have a more difficult time with her.

Robert pondered the best way to approach telling his children about their relationship. He decided to call them and just tell them that he had started to date. He called Jonas first and started the conversation on a light note. Then there was a long pause, and Jonas picked up on it immediately. He asked Robert whether there was something he wanted to talk about. Robert proceeded to tell his son that he had started dating, and Jonas responded, sounding somewhat relieved, that he was pleased to hear that Robert was making a life for himself. Jonas did not ask his father for a lot of details about the woman he was dating, for which Robert was relieved. He would save that for another conversation.

Well, one hurdle was behind him. Now he had to call Samantha. Robert pondered a moment. How could he do this and be very sensitive to her feelings about her mother? He decided there was no easy way and that he just had to take the bull by the horns and do it. So he called. She answered the phone and they began chatting. Then he told her that he had something important to discuss with her, and then he paused.

Surprising Robert, she came right out and asked him if he had found someone. Quietly, he just said yes. She haltingly asked him to tell her about the woman. Robert had not expected this response. He found himself beginning to chatter away, describing Jan, her appearance, and her personality. He told her that Jan and he were just having a nice time together, getting to know each other and enjoying each other's company.

Samantha asked her father whether he had slept in her mother's bed with Jan. Fortunately, Robert could answer honestly. No, he said. They slept together at Jan's house. Robert then told Samantha that he expected her to have mixed feelings about his dating, and she acknowledged that. But he said that he felt it was better to be honest and direct and keep the lines of communication open, and that he did not expect her to be friends with this woman at first. But maybe over time she would be open to at least meeting her, Robert continued. He acknowledged that she had had a very close relationship to her mother and knew she would be appropriately protective of her mother's memory. Robert said he would try to be understanding and respect Samantha's position, and that he would wait until she said she was ready to meet Jan.

Robert and Jan continued to date. Jan soon introduced Robert to her children, since they lived in town. She knew the process would be easier with her children because they had a father who had remarried and they had already been introduced to previous men in Jan's life. At the meeting the children were pleasant. One son was friendly, and the other was more standoffish and protective of Jan. Robert understood his position and was respectful of the son's feelings. He hoped that in time the son would be more receptive to him. But Robert was prepared to be patient.

After taking Jan to New York for a weekend to meet his son, Robert's next challenge was to introduce Jan to his daughter. How could he introduce her to Samantha in a nonthreatening way? Robert thought about it, discussed it with Jan, and also asked his late wife's good friend. She suggested that they meet in a neutral place where Robert had not traveled with his late wife. What a good suggestion, he thought, and planned just such a getaway weekend in Santa Barbara.

Robert had distant cousins in Santa Barbara whom he had not seen in a while. He thought it would be nice to go and spend a week there. Samantha could fly down for a long weekend, and he would put them all up at a bed-and-breakfast. They could play golf, hike the trails of Montecito, visit a nearby artists' community in the Santa Ynez mountains, and picnic in the city's botanical gardens.

The weekend visit with Samantha was fairly smooth. However, at one point Samantha started crying and admitted how hard the weekend was for her. She admitted it was especially difficult because Jan was such a nice woman that she could not hate her. Robert felt strong emotion for his daughter. At that moment, he just hugged her long and hard. Jan was smart enough to go for a walk and give them time to talk. The final day of the trip, Jan suggested that Robert spend the afternoon with his daughter alone. It was a good suggestion. They took a long walk and had a small picnic. They talked. Samantha admitted that Santa Barbara was an exquisite spot, and she was sad that her mother could not be a part of the adventure. Robert nodded in agreement. He noted that no one had wanted her mother to die and told her that he also wished she were still alive and there with them.

Robert then told her how hard it had been to make the decision to date. He also noted that his relationship with Jan was very different from his relationship with her mother. He and her mother had grown together during their marriage, while Jan and he were at a later stage of life when they met, so it was a comfortable relationship, a safe relationship for two people in midlife who were striving to find ways to adjust to major loss and start a new chapter in their lives. Robert explained that both he and Jan were realistic about the opportunities that lay ahead for them. They were looking to each other for companionship and hoped to spend their later years together, taking care of each other.

Robert let his daughter know that he would always be there for her and that she need not feel afraid that she would emotionally lose him. She nodded, knowing that he would indeed be there for her, but that she would lose him anyway. She knew that in fact that is how life works and that she would adjust in time.

Robert and Jan continued their relationship. A year later they made plans to formally begin a new chapter of their lives together. But first Robert needed to finish some old business.

Robert needed to go to the cemetery and visit his late wife's grave. He told her about Jan and their life together. He thanked her for her blessings—their wonderful life together and their two beautiful children—and promised he would treasure their legacy as he moved forward with Jan to carve the next chapter of his life. He then said good-bye. Wiping his tears, he left her grave site without looking back. There was a lightness in his stride as he looked forward to the new life he and Jan would build together.

QUESTIONS ABOUT ROBERT'S STORY

1. Can you identify the stages in Robert's adjustment journey?

   _____

   _____

   _____

   _____

2. Contrast his journey with Tina's.

   a. What aspects are similar?

   _____

   _____

   _____

   _____

   b. What aspects are different?

   _____

   _____

   _____

   _____

3. Robert's adjustment process is typical of a man's experience following his wife's death. How do you think his adjustment might be different from that of a woman? How is his experience different from or similar to yours?

   _____

   _____

   _____

   _____

4. Can you identify with Robert's story or Tina's story? Which parts?

   _____

   _____

   _____

   _____

Chapter 9

Ruth's Story and Johanna's Story

The thesis of the three-stage model is that you have two choices in your adjustment journey: either you can make accommodations for your loss in your life, or you can choose to date, eventually connect with a new partner, and begin a qualitatively new chapter in your life. In this chapter I present two of many possible stories of the older widow's experience.

While Tina's tale, the story of a young widow told in chapter 7, is an example of how someone connects with a new partner and begins a new chapter in her life, the following two stories echo fairly common tales of older widows whose spouses have died. Older women of today do not always reconnect and create a new structure of meaning in their life. Instead they make many compromises. The two stories that follow illustrate some of the compromises older women appear to make.

RUTH'S STORY

Ruth and Richard met and married while they were both in college. As was common at the time she went directly from living in her mother's home to living in her husband's home. Ruth taught middle-school English for five years while Richard began his business. When they began their family, Ruth quit teaching and raised her children. Later, while her children were in middle school, Ruth went back to school, got a master's degree, and began tutoring children with learning disabilities at home. Ruth liked being at home when her children returned from school.

After Ruth's children went to college Ruth worked out of the house, making her own schedule so that she could meet friends for lunch. She and Richard had a group of coupled friends with whom they socialized, and Ruth kept in touch with her sister and brother, who lived in nearby communities. Ruth was quite content with her life.

Ruth's children married shortly after college. Her two daughters married men from their hometown, and her son met a young woman while he was working in New York and settled in a New York suburban community. All of Ruth's children were settling in, buying houses, starting families. Ruth loved being involved with her grandchildren, and she relished every Sunday morning when her older daughter would come with the grandchildren for brunch.

Then, while Ruth and Richard were on vacation during the summer she turned seventy, Richard collapsed. Ruth took him to the nearby emergency room, where she found out that he had a massive coronary. He was placed on life support for a few days, and then he died.

Ruth was numb and in shock. Her daughters flew to be with their mother and accompany her and their father's body back to their hometown. Ruth has little recollection about this trip home.

Everyone gathered at the family home. The funeral was a blur; everything happened so quickly. After the funeral Ruth looked around and took stock of her situation. Financially she would be okay, she realized, but what was she going to do with her life? She did not know. She and Richard had been in transition—they were considering buying a condominium in a warmer climate, perhaps South Carolina or Georgia. But when Richard died, Ruth's world had stopped. Their plans for the next phase of their life halted. What had seemed stable, even, and predictable was now in flux. Ruth no longer had plans.

She knew she needed to take one step at a time. She knew Richard would have wanted her to make a life for herself, but what she would do, she did not know. So she merely got up in the morning, spoke to her daughter (she called every morning to check on her), had coffee, and began her day, which consisted of getting dressed, writing notes of acknowledgment, and then staring into space. Friends often called and asked her to breakfast, lunch, and dinner. Sometimes she accepted, but sometimes she refused.

Ruth was not sleeping. Nighttime became her enemy. She tossed and turned, and she could not even concentrate enough to read. She knew that she was in bad shape. One friend suggested that she ask her doctor for some medicine to help her sleep. In talking to her friends she was surprised to find out how many were taking antianxiety medicines or antidepressants. Ruth thought that a visit to her doctor was a good idea. Another friend suggested that Ruth start sleeping in a different bedroom, in a smaller bed, where she wouldn't be reminded of her loss.

Days rolled into weeks; weeks became months. Ruth gradually developed a routine—she found that if she spoke to her daughter in the morning, had her coffee, and then went to exercise, she felt good and was comforted by having at least some structure to her day.

Before Richard's death, Ruth had been tutoring children with learning disabilities in her home. At this point she was not totally able to concentrate yet, so she did not start tutoring again. Instead, she took a month off. She thought about her work and realized that working from her home was too isolating. She needed to leave the house and go somewhere to work. So she thought about her options.

She made appointments at the private schools in the community and talked to the principals about her possibly tutoring part-time. One principal also asked if she would be interested in substituting, but she decided that working all day was too much for her. She thanked the principal for his offer but said that she was only interested in tutoring.

Eventually Ruth found a school where she could tutor students. She made arrangements to be there two afternoons a week, and she also saw a few students at her house another few afternoons a week. So she now had some structure to her life.

Her daughter suggested that Ruth find a new hobby or activity to start. Ruth had always wanted to paint, and she had heard that the community senior center was offering a class on drawing and painting from the right side of the brain, so she decided to enroll. She also started taking bridge lessons with some friends, since she had played bridge in college and was interested in starting up again.

Ruth looked at her schedule. She now had some work, a drawing and painting class, and bridge lessons. In addition, Ruth had to focus on the business aspects of her husband's estate. Lawyers were facilitating the sale of Richard's insurance agency to his partner, but there were papers to sign and calls to return. That seemed like enough activity for her.

In time Ruth and her older daughter went to pick out the memorial stone. This was a hard task. Ruth realized that she was also selecting the stone for her own grave, since she would be buried next to Richard. The stone was also a final confirmation that her husband was dead. It took several days for Ruth to get over this experience.

Several months later Ruth's daughter decided to take her mother out for the afternoon to have lunch and go shopping. At lunch they began talking.

Ruth's daughter asked her mother what she envisioned for herself down the road. She responded that at present she was just taking one day at a time, although the days were going faster and she was being more productive with her time. For the first time in a long while, she told her daughter, she was coming home and feeling a good kind of tired, and she was now sleeping regularly.

Ruth's daughter asked her mother whether she thought about her future. Ruth looked at her daughter in a funny way. Her daughter asked whether she wanted to stay in the house or move to smaller quarters. Did she want an apartment with a doorman and other amenities so that she would not have to come home to a dark, empty house each night?

Ruth stopped to think. Did she want to move? Right now she was at home with the memories. In time she would consider selling and moving somewhere else. Perhaps she would take the next year to sort through stuff and get the house ready to be put on the market. That activity would provide her with the impetus to go through her husband's things.

Then Ruth's daughter asked her if she wanted to go to the beach in the summer to be with the grandchildren—Ruth's two daughters usually rented a condo at a shore community in the summer for two weeks. Yes, Ruth would like to come along.

Finally, Ruth's daughter took a big breath and asked her mother whether she planned to date. Ruth was astounded and taken aback, and then she got angry. How dare her daughter bring up such a subject? Then she calmed down and spoke to her daughter in a calm, even tone. No, she was not planning to date. She did not even want to think about dating. She had decided she would build a life around her daughters and grandchildren. Her work would give structure to her day, and her daughters would be her anchors. As her grandchildren grew, she would take them on special trips. Yes, Ruth was quite sure she did not want to make a life for herself with another man.

Despite her outburst, it had been a good afternoon. After the initial shock, Ruth was glad that her daughter had broached the subject. It was helpful for Ruth to be able to state her expectations to her daughter, and as she stated them aloud, she felt better.

Ruth is an example of a woman who decides not to look for a new companion after the death of her spouse. Instead she makes accommodations for her loss and stays connected to her adult children whom she will use as her anchors. Hers is a fairly conventional and traditional approach to widowhood. More and more frequently I hear about widowed women young and old who are still interested in finding a male companion. Johanna's story is an example of this kind of adjustment.

QUESTIONS ABOUT RUTH'S ADJUSTMENT

1. Identify the stages of Ruth's adjustment.

_____

_____

_____

_____

2. Did Ruth experience intrapsychic change? How can you tell?

_____

_____

_____

_____

3. Do you identify with Ruth's journey? How?

_____

_____

_____

_____

JOHANNA'S STORY

Johanna was in her late sixties. Her husband of forty-six years had died suddenly from a heart attack two months before. Yes, he had had a heart condition, but Johanna had never believed that the heart condition would be so severe as to end his life so soon. Everyone said he was fine and would live for years with his heart condition. Well, he lived two years, no more. And Johanna was appreciative of having that time together. But now he was dead and Johanna was very sad.

Johanna and her husband were college sweethearts. They married in their senior year of college, graduated together, grew up together, had children together. They were together for their children's sports activities, dance recitals, graduations, and marriages. However, now she had to face everything alone. Her husband of almost fifty years was gone!

Johanna knew she was numb and in shock. She had trouble getting out of bed each morning. She had to pinch herself to be sure that she was awake and not in a dream—or rather a nightmare. Her husband's side of the bed was empty and would forever stay that way—not like when he had been in the hospital and would come home in a few days. No, this was forever and comprehending forever was hard. This whole experience seemed surreal.

Johanna hardly remembered the funeral. She hardly remembered the people—lots of people attending, hugging her, kidding her, shaking her hand. People she knew and people she did not know all wishing her well. It was all a blur. Then there was the meal after the funeral. The food tasted like sand; it was hard to swallow. And then more visitors. The time seemed endless, and at the same time the event seemed to last just a nanosecond before it was all over.

Now Johanna was alone—very alone. The funeral was over, her children had gone back to their homes, and Johanna had to start making a life for herself. But just the idea seemed overwhelming—so overwhelming that she became paralyzed. So in the morning she got up, poured herself some coffee, and went back to bed. Friends called, but she just let the answering machine take the calls. She did not have the energy to talk on the phone. Maybe she would feel different later on in the day. For now coffee and toast was all she could muster.

Later that day she did answer the phone. It was a friend asking to meet her for lunch. She accepted without thinking about it. Lunch, breakfast, dinner—it did not matter. All food tasted the same to her, and she did not have an appetite anyway. At lunch her friend chattered. Johanna listened at first but then she could not listen anymore and just spaced out. When Johanna found herself listening again she could tell that she had not missed much. When they were done, her friend insisted on paying, wanting to be kind and generous and needing to relieve her feelings of guilt and relief that it was Johanna's husband who had died and not hers. Johanna understood. She also wished it had not been her husband.

Johanna went home. She knew that she would face a long evening alone, but it was better than expending energy making small talk and being with friends. She was not ready to socialize. First she had to face her accountant and lawyer and deal with the concrete issues of money and the estate.

When Johanna saw the accountant and the lawyer, she found it was easier than she had expected to deal with the concrete financial and legal issues. She now knew how much she would have to live on monthly. That information helped. And the lawyer and accountant were kind and caring. It felt good to have some male kindness.

But when she got in her car outside the lawyer's office, she broke down. She was quite sad. She realized that in the future the only men who would care for her were people who were paid to take care of her; no man would necessarily help her out of love.

So Johanna stood back and made an assessment of who was still in her corner and on whom she could count. She knew that she could count on her children, but she did not want to burden them. She knew that she could count on her friends and their husbands, but she did not want to wear out her welcome. It was at that moment that she realized that she was from a generation of women who for the most part had been taken care of by their spouses, and here she was, quite aware of the fact that she might never be taken care of by a spouse again. The revelation was quite overwhelming. Johanna knew she was strong and somewhat independent, perfectly capable of handling most matters. But there had always been a safety net—her husband. She might have followed her own path, but she had valued, even depended on, his perspective. Now he was gone. She would have to handle everything herself.

Johanna was age sixty-eight, too old and yet young. Too old probably to find a new mate much later down the road, and yet young enough to conceivably live a very long time alone. Alone. What would it be like to live alone? She had no idea. She had been married for almost fifty years.

Fortunately, the initial few months were filled with paperwork—writing acknowledgments, estate documents, medical insurance forms regarding her husband's illness. The paperwork had to be done, and she did it. But then the paperwork was complete; she had nothing that had to be done. She knew she could have lunch or dinner with friends, but it did not meet her needs nor did it help her feel better.

Her friends had suggested that she participate in an activity, but nothing seemed enticing to her. She knew she needed to begin to decide what to do with her life—she needed to do something—but she could not even concentrate enough to read a book or watch a movie. She loved music but now she found herself crying when she listened to her favorite pieces. She knew she needed to move forward, but at the same time she felt stuck.

A friend suggested that she talk to her doctor about antidepressant medication. After all, she was obviously depressed. Her feet felt like lead. Food tasted like sawdust. She had no appetite or motivation to get out of bed. She awoke at four o'clock every morning and tossed and turned. Then a second friend suggested that an antidepressant might decrease her anxiety and let her sleep, which would in turn help her heal by resetting her body clock (Wehr et al. 1979).

Without further ado Johanna made an appointment to see her physician. She agreed that a little medicine would help her get over the hump. She prescribed the medicines and Johanna began taking them. To her surprise, within a week she felt much better. She noticed that she was even smiling. Maybe there was hope. Maybe she could feel better. Maybe she could create a future for herself. After all, if she felt better physically, it would be easier for her to make a new life for herself.

As the days passed and her energy increased, she looked forward to spring and being able to stay outdoors. She looked forward to the opportunity to play tennis, which would be a wonderful way to spend time with people. She could take tennis lessons and focus on improving her serve over the summer. For Johanna, life was looking more positive.

Months went by and before she knew it, there was a rhythm to her life. On Monday and Wednesday afternoons, she played mah-jongg; on Tuesday and Thursday afternoons, she played tennis. Friday was her own day, but on Saturday, she had lunch with friends. Sunday afternoons she attended concerts once a month, and on Saturday or Sunday evenings, she had dinner out with friends.

Home alone, Johanna puttered with her plants, watched TV, and tended to her mail. Friends kept telling her that she needed to start a new activity but she did not know what activity to try. Moreover, she was content with her life for the time being. She decided she would take six more months to coast before asking some difficult questions of herself and facing some hard choices, such as whether to sell the house and what activities to try.

Six months came and went, and Johanna's schedule did not change. When winter came she had to stop playing tennis outdoors, so she had two free afternoons a week. She had made herself a deal that she would find a place to volunteer her services or find a part-time job so that she would have something more concrete she could look forward to. Her friend ran a gift basket business, so she would see if she could help her friend at Christmastime. Since Johanna had worked in marketing before she retired, she thought maybe she could help her friend expand her business.

At lunch one day, Johanna and a friend were talking, and this friend asked Johanna if she had thought about dating—something she had worked very hard to avoid thinking about. At first, she had thought that she would not date; she could not replace her husband. Then she wondered who would want to date her. A man her age would want a woman in her early sixties. So that would leave only men in their seventies and eighties, infirm or fairly dependent. She knew she did not want to take care of another sick husband.

Part of what had made Johanna so sad after her husband's death, she told her friend, was the thought that she would have to live the next thirty years alone without a male companion. Her friend stopped her, asking why Johanna thought that if she dated she had to have a permanent partner? Perhaps she could just go on an occasional date or have a non-live-in companion. Johanna had never thought a man would be interested in that.

Johanna thanked her friend. She said she would definitely rethink the dating issue and consider going out with some men. Her friend seemed pleased and said she would pass her name around.

Walking away from the restaurant, Johanna cringed. Dating? Ugh! She had not dated since adolescence, and times had changed. She could not imagine having sex with a man other than her husband. He had accepted her settling lumps, increasing cellulite, and wrinkles. They could laugh about their changing bodies because they had watched each other grow and change. But making love to another man? What a ridiculous thought. She could not go there just yet. She would have to give herself time to adjust to the thought of dating first.

Where would she meet someone to date? She would do fine with word of mouth. It would be much easier than using the Internet. She knew plenty of people. She would just let them know that she was available.

Home alone, she casually looked through her wardrobe. What would she wear on this phantom date? She imagined having dinner and interviewing this phantom man. What would she say to him? What would she ask him? She called a friend of hers who had been widowed a couple of years before, and asked for some dating pointers.

Johanna reviewed the conversation. The first things that she would want to know were what this man was like and what he did with his time. Then she would ask about his family, his former wife, and his children. Then she would want to know his intentions—was he just looking to play the field or did he want a relationship? She knew she could not believe everything he said but it would be a starting point and a relief for the moment. In the process she would be able to learn how he thought about life, his perspective on the world.

Knowing what she would say on a date, Johanna was more comfortable about the dating issue. Johanna decided she could call some people and begin to spread the word that she might be interested in meeting men.

As time passed and spring arrived, Johanna found that she felt even better. The medicine definitely helped and she was making at least one plan a week to do things. She had lunch with friends, occasionally went to the symphony, and carefully selected upbeat movies to see. As the weather warmed up she started going to the tennis courts to practice her serve. She could focus on the sun, flowers, sky, and clouds. She could set goals to see whether her serve would improve. At the end of the day she would come home and feel tired from the physical exercise.

She joined a ladies tennis group and soon people began calling asking her to be part of a doubles game. She was delighted—she had developed a social life. As the summer progressed, Johanna was aware that her world was expanding and had some useful structure to it. She was beginning to move forward with a new life.

One day, the phone rang. She was surprised to hear a male voice on the other end. It turned out that a friend had given this man, Arthur, a recent widower, her name and number.

"Would she like to go out and have dinner together?" he asked.

Johanna was surprised. Was it that easy? "Of course," she replied. "I would be delighted to meet you and have dinner."

Johanna put down the phone and was stunned. I have not been out on a date since I was an adolescent, she thought, more than forty years ago. Now she felt like an adolescent all over again and at the same time an old woman. What should she wear? What would she say? How would she behave? Where would he take her?

It has been so long since she had thought about such things. She was not quite sure how she would proceed. First she'd choose an appropriate outfit, she decided. It was a Sunday night date so she would wear a nice pair of slacks, a sweater, and a scarf, but no jewelry.

Johanna stopped to think about her phantom interview. Now she would be able to put it to work. She thought she'd begin by asking him to talk about himself, his wife, and their life together. As she rehearsed their conversation, Johanna realized what was making her so anxious: the *idea* of going out on a date. So she told herself to just think about the evening as a time to get to know a potential new friend. That was it. With that approach she knew she would do much better.

Sunday evening arrived quickly. Johanna took extra time to prepare herself for the date. She looked beautiful, she thought as she admired herself in the mirror, not bad for an older woman.

Johanna answered the door and was pleasantly surprised to see a young-looking man in his seventies standing there. He introduced himself in a gentlemanly manner, helped her on with her wrap, and opened the door of the car for her.

As they drove, Johanna talked about inconsequential things—the pleasant weather, the nice restaurant he was taking her to, the food the restaurant serves. They arrived at the restaurant and were seated at a quiet table for two. Conversation flowed and the waiter's visits to the table seemed to be an annoying intrusion instead of a welcome interruption. Surprised at how comfortable she felt with Arthur, Johanna knew she was having a good time. Arthur also seemed animated, so she knew that he was enjoying the evening as well.

Over dinner Johanna and Arthur exchanged stories. He described his life with his wife, her illness, and her subsequent death. He told her about his children and described his activities, and she listened carefully to see if there was common ground.

Next Johanna told him about her life, her activities, her likes, and her dislikes. She told him about her marriage to her husband, his heart condition, and his subsequent death. Johanna had not realized how comforting it would be to talk with someone with a similar history.

The waiter brought the check and the dinner came to a close. "What will happen next?" Johanna wondered. She didn't have to wait long to find out, because Arthur immediately asked whether she would like an encore. Johanna was surprised at the ease with which he broached the issue, also a bit surprised at her quick response—she accepted.

When he took Johanna home, he did not make an overture to kiss her good night. Rather, he walked her to her door, saying he had had a lovely evening and would call in a few days. Johanna was relieved at how easy the ending was.

Home alone, the door shut, Johanna pondered the evening's conversation, the man, his attributes, and his situation. She thought about how easy it had been for her to go on a date and talk to a strange man. But she would not analyze the evening, she told herself. Rather she would accept the evening as just a night out and move on to her plans for the next day.

The next morning Johanna called the friend who had given Arthur her number to report on the date. Instead of giving out all the details thus destroying the intimacy of the evening, she merely thanked her friend, saying that she had had a wonderful time and that she would go out with him again.

Johanna was pleased at the way she had handled the whole event. She planned her week knowing that she now had a new dimension to her life.

Three days later Arthur called and asked Johanna out again. Johanna said yes and thus began her first extended dating experience. After a few weeks, she noticed that she was tackling her work projects with a gusto and enthusiasm she had had difficulty mustering before she met Arthur. She was surprised at the new spring in her step and the ease with which her day got started. She had been unaware of how deep her depression was before this new aspect in her life developed—male companionship. Before Arthur entered her life, she had dismissed her lethargy as a normal part of aging. Now she realized it was depression.

Johanna was having a wonderful time enjoying Arthur's company. He was a pleasant man, kind and gentle, very different from her husband, so she had to learn to mesh with a different kind of personality. Despite the effort involved, she was actually relieved at the differences between him and her late husband. They decreased the unconscious familiarity that would stir up memories and lessened her feelings of guilt about dating.

Johanna and Arthur became physically intimate several months after they started dating. It was a particularly difficult moment for Johanna. She knew she could be a widow the rest of her life, or she could enter the world of looking for male company, sleeping with another man or perhaps more than one man. Was she prepared for that? She was not sure. She was not even prepared to consider that possibility. Right now she would just think about being with Arthur, she decided.

The relationship, which was very comfortable, was also growing. Johanna enjoyed their dates. They went to movies, the theater, museums. On one occasion they stayed at a bed-and-breakfast in a nearby city for the weekend. After a time, Arthur began spending the night. Then he extended the night to the weekend. Johanna enjoyed his extended visits, but she found that she also liked it when he went home and she had time to herself again.

After several months, just as Johanna was settling into this new mode, she received a phone call from Arthur, who said he did not feel well and was on his way to his doctor's office. Would she be there for him if he needed her?

Stunned, Johanna said yes. After she hung up, she started thinking. Of course she would be there for him, whatever that meant. But Johanna felt a little unsettled, a little scared, and ashamedly a little angry about this new development. She had just finished caring for her ailing husband, and she was just starting to have fun again. She did not want to start caretaking again. Her ruminations were interrupted by the phone ringing.

It was Arthur—his doctor was sending him to the hospital. Apologetically but anxiously, Arthur asked if Johanna would come and wait with him, and without hesitation Johanna agreed, saying she would meet him at the hospital.

Later that day, Arthur was admitted to a room in the hospital, with Johanna by his side. When the doctor arrived, Johanna got up to leave, but Arthur asked her to stay. The doctor informed Arthur that although additional tests had been scheduled, he was 90 percent sure Arthur would need a stent, which would require a minor surgical procedure.

After the doctor left, Arthur turned to Johanna and said that he knew this was a lot for Johanna to endure—after all, she had just finished being a caregiver to her husband with major heart disease. He asked her what she wanted to do. Johanna was stunned; she had not expected that question. Without hesitation, Johanna said she thought they should handle this medical crisis first, and then figure out where to go from there. Arthur nodded. It seemed like a sensible and rational plan.

Johanna sat with Arthur while he called his children and told them about the problem. The children, grown adults living in other cities, asked whether Arthur wanted them to come immediately. Arthur said no and asked them to just stand by.

Johanna, feeling drained, stood up to leave the hospital. She knew it was time for her to go home and relax. She gently kissed Arthur good-bye and told him she would see him the next day.

Johanna knew she was not prepared to nurse another man to health. She considered her options. She did not have to marry Arthur. She did not even have to live with him. The question was, would that meet her needs? Could she be content that way? Was she prepared to break up with Arthur? She was not sure. One risk was that she would be alone the rest of her life. On the other hand, she might meet someone in better health and they could make a life together.

Johanna decided to sleep on it. She did not have to make a decision now; she would wait until Arthur had undergone the procedure and they had more information about his condition. She knew that, although the procedure Arthur needed was simple, complications could arise as a result of it. She'd have to wait and see what happened. Right now Johanna knew she needed to get some sleep.

The following day, Johanna awoke feeling refreshed. Her world seemed surreal and she wondered whether she had dreamt that Arthur was ill. Then she snapped back to reality. She poured herself a cup of coffee and called Arthur to check on him. She told him that she had some errands to run and would come to the hospital to visit him later in the day. Arthur told her that his children would also be there later that day. Johanna was pleased and relieved. It was truly his children's place, not Johanna's, to be with their father and to assume responsibility for any medical decisions that needed to be made.

The next few days were busy. Johanna got up in the morning, checked with the hospital, ran her errands, and then went to visit Arthur. The routine felt familiar, but she knew it was different. Arthur had his operation and was scheduled to go back to his home. Johanna knew that there was an unasked question on the table. Fortunately, Arthur's daughter took the reins and offered to stay an extra week to take care of him. The question no longer had to be answered, at least for the moment.

The dynamics were in place. Arthur would go home to his house and his daughter would orchestrate the care for a week. When she left, Johanna would coordinate any further care. So Johanna did not have to make any long-term decisions; she could make decisions one week at a time.

Over time, Arthur healed. He recuperated at his own home, and Johanna helped coordinate his care. On occasion she stayed at Arthur's home. Many evenings they had dinner together and had serious discussions about their relationship. They also talked openly about the limits of her responsibility. Arthur was appreciative of Johanna's care and help.

Arthur asked Johanna whether she would consider traveling with him to someplace warm where he could continue to recuperate. Johanna said yes, and they began making plans for an extended trip. Thus, one day at a time, the character of the relationship defined itself. An overall policy statement was not necessary.

Johanna and Arthur continued their relationship. Because of Arthur's illness, she decided that she did not want to marry Arthur, but that she would be his permanent companion. Arthur, in turn, was delighted to have Johanna's support and companionship. He did not push the issue of marriage or living together.

How did their children feel about the relationship? They were happy that their parents had a significant companion, and they understood why Johanna and Arthur had decided not to marry. When the children came into town, both Johanna and Arthur together would spend time with them. When Arthur visited his children in their respective cities, he would go alone, and Johanna did the same.

Johanna and Arthur's arrangement is one that seems to be growing more popular with people in their sixties, seventies, and even eighties. As people are living longer, more people look to these kinds of pragmatic solutions to meet their need for companionship while bypassing the logistical, legal, and financial complications that can come with marriage. These older couples know that their life expectancy is limited, and so they try to enjoy the moment as best they can.

QUESTIONS ABOUT JOHANNA'S ADJUSTMENT

1. Identify the stages of the adjustment journey in Johanna's story.

_____

_____

_____

_____

2. Contrast Johanna's adjustment with Ruth's.

_____

_____

_____

_____

3. Did Johanna go through intrapsychic change? How do you know?

_____

_____

_____

_____

4. Do you identify with the character in either story? If so, with whom? How? Why?

_____

_____

_____

_____

5. Identify your own concerns as you move through the stages of your journey.

_____

_____

_____

_____

6. How do you think you can tackle your concerns?

_____

_____

_____

_____

Postscript

Tina's, Robert's, Ruth's, and Johanna's stories are touching and real. As I travel the country, I hear stories like theirs, with variations, almost daily. They provide a useful model for the adjustment process of young and old widows and widowers. The stories of Tina, Robert, Ruth, and Johanna illustrate the two major themes of this book, namely that your spouse is your anchor, and that the adjustment after death of a spouse appears to take place in stages. I have written this workbook in order to introduce you to those stages and familiarize you with the tasks and skills you need to accomplish in each stage so you can move on to the next stage of adjustment.

TIME LINE

Returning to old activities, practices, or habits from the past may personally empower you and give you the initial impetus to make the changes necessary to recraft your life. Life is about three things: love, work, and play. The degree to which each of these areas is working for you is likely related to the level of satisfaction and happiness in your life. To find out how well these areas are working in your life, go to the next page and complete the time line chart. During each decade of your life, what significant things did you do in each category, that is, in your love, work, and play activities? After you fill out the chart, look at it carefully. During each stage, what made your life successful for you, and what made it satisfying? (Note: Feelings of success and satisfaction don't always result from the same activity.) Now, as you go through your current life transition, is there anything from the past that you can fall back on to achieve more satisfaction or success?

Time Line		
	Love	Work	Play
20s			
30s			
40s			
50s			
60s			
70s			
80s			

You are now at the conclusion of the book. To assess the value this book has had for you, answer the questions below.

1. Have you learned anything that you did not know before you started reading this book? If so, list those things below.

_____

_____

_____

2. Do you have a useful mental framework for the process of adjustment after major loss?

   a. What is your understanding of the framework?

   _____

   _____

   b. How does it differ from your previous notions about adjustment?

   _____

   _____

3. Name one thing you have begun to do differently in your daily life since beginning to read the book.

_____

_____

The chapters on pseudoequilibrium and transition to liftoff present particularly difficult concepts. Do not expect to understand and internalize those concepts on the first reading. You may need to read the descriptions of the internal dynamic growth process more than once.

In my work, I have discovered that the three-stage model is timeless. As the baby boom population ages and people reach the stage of life where spouses often die, more and more people are facing this adjustment process. But no matter what decade or century we're in, the basic principles continue to apply. The major variations on the theme come with the increasing number of ways elderly people, both men and women, accommodate their losses and create new lifestyle approaches.

So where do you, the reader, go from here? You now have the framework for adjustment. You know your own particular lifestyle. You have to decide what you want to try in the next part of your life transition. When you try something new and it works, great. If it does not work, do not stop; regroup and try something else.

As I stated in the introduction, I wrote this book as a response to widowed people who came up to me and said, "Please tell me what to do to move on with my life now that my spouse has died." This book tells you what to do. Be aware of your feelings, but know that you don't have to act on them, particularly if they are destructive or self-defeating. Act based on your cognitive thoughts. As a result you will find your actions are more constructive and deliberate.

WHERE MY JOURNEY HAS TAKEN ME

Now I would like to share with you some of the changes I experienced in my adjustment to widowhood.

It has been more than a decade since my husband became ill and died. At that time, I had two adolescent sons at home, one about to leave for college. I lived in a comfortable suburban home. I belonged to a country club, where I played golf. Like many of the women of my peer group, I had a career—a psychotherapy practice. I had friends.

Right after my husband died, I continued my practice. I went to the country club and joined several women's golf groups. My married friends included me on weekend outings. Three months after my husband died I took my children on a trip to Canada so that we could regroup before my older son left for college.

When my older son left home, our family of four was now a family of two. My younger son retreated to his bedroom, as many adolescent boys do. In his case it was for self-protection. He no longer had two other people in the family to cushion him and to give him some distance from me, which he needed as he went through the normal developmental process of separating from home.

During the first year after my husband's death, I reached out to single friends and began to go with them on social outings. I looked to them to tell me what the singles scene was like. I did not have much free time to explore new activities or adventures, but I was curious. Most of the time I spent doing paperwork and tending my practice.

After the first year, though, my close married friends began to shy away from including me in couples outings. I was expected to move on with my life. Fortunately, my golf groups and my one new activity, bridge, gave me the social interaction I needed for a while. Women were kind and asked to fix me up. I dated and began a relationship, which eventually fizzled. Then I had to start the hard task of recrafting my life.

At that point I was ready to revisit the difficult year when my husband was ill. I mourned his death and the daily traumas we had experienced in dealing with his illness. I decided to memorialize him by planting a garden at his alma mater, the University of Pennsylvania. In addition, I donated a gardening encyclopedia to my younger son's private high school. My husband had been an avid gardener and I thought the garden would bring beauty to the world each spring and be a small reminder of what had been important to my husband. Today my older son is the caretaker of the garden at the university, now his alma mater, and he makes sure that it continues to flourish.

Another major transition awaited me soon after I planted the garden: my younger son was about to graduate from high school and leave home, and I was about to go back to school for my third graduate degree—a practical necessity and also a diversion that would keep me from noticing the echoes in my large, suddenly empty home. I decided to get a dog both for protection and for company. Heidi, a sweet German shepherd, became a warm addition to my life. Children coming to see me for therapy loved Heidi, and Heidi always thought the children were coming to visit her, not me.

At that point, my financial adviser suggested that I think about selling my house. For monetary reasons, I had to make a decision to either leave the country club or sell my house. I decided to keep the house. During this transition period in my sons' lives, I felt it important to keep the family home so that they would have a familiar place to return to during their breaks. I would not have time to play golf and use the club while in school anyway, so I left the country club.

I attended graduate school in another city, Washington, D.C., where I met a delightful mix of women undergoing midlife career transitions. It gave a new focus to my world and allowed me to disengage from my traditional suburban social life in which I did not easily fit because I was now single.

My children continued to include me in their lives. My younger son kindly introduced me to his college friends' parents, who included me in school-related social events and exposed me to a different population, expanding my horizons. At the same time my older son went abroad for a year, and I had the pleasure of joining him in Scotland. He and I then traveled to Paris for his twenty-first birthday, another growing experience for me. He also introduced me to his college friends and I was quite flattered to be included in this part of his life. Certainly, my children were my transitional anchors.

During this period of time, I dated some and had another relationship, not as intense as the first relationship, which also fizzled in time. I decided then that I would be very careful before I connected to anyone else again. The pain of these losses was not worth the short-term pleasures.

I traveled with single women friends. I went to Florida to visit my mentor, a kind woman. I played golf; I had wonderful weekend adventures in other cities; I went to visit my children in college. Then, one weekend, my younger son gave me the privilege and pleasure of entertaining his school's very famous vocal group, the Whiffenpoofs, during their spring break. It was a lot of fun. Into my house walked a group of fifteen young men. They were starved; the lasagna and turkey I had fixed lasted thirty minutes and then I was out of food. The young men spread their sleeping bags and computers around my house. The house was full. The conversation was exciting and stimulating and the students gave two outstanding concerts, an informal one in my home and a more formal one at a nearby country club. The next morning I went to a bagel shop and got bags of bagels and several copies of *The New York Times*. The college men and I sat around my dining room table and talked before they took off. It was a transition point for me. My life was rich, even though I did not have a man. I knew I was okay.

Around the same time, I was invited to go on a blind, double date, which had been arranged by the wife of one of my husband's closest childhood friends. After the concert we all attended, I invited my date, Phillip, back to my house for coffee and dessert. I was amazed at how interesting he was. He was very different from anyone I had ever met before. My heart was cautious, but my head told me not to dismiss this man. A therapist friend had wisely told me that you can learn all you need to know about a person on the first date, so I interviewed him carefully. He told me about his prior life, his family, and his work. That was a lot to learn on a first date, but the time went quickly and we were enjoying ourselves. When the date ended, I knew he would call again. I was not in a hurry; my life was busy and full and I would be patient.

Indeed, he did call again, and we started dating. We did lots of wonderful new activities together. We went to arboretums, art museums, movies, and cafés, for walks and bike rides. We learned about each other on all fronts. It was a new experience for me; I became very comfortable with him and began to like him a lot. My mother found this man delightful and charming. She was thrilled; she knew he was good for me. When I asked why, she pointed out that I was no longer running from activity to activity. I seemed to be content in a way that I had not before. I stopped in my tracks. My mother was right.

Well, Phillip and I developed a relationship. He took me to Los Angeles, California to meet his wonderful family, and then he took me to meet more cousins in Santa Barbara, California, a city that has since captured my heart. We spent time figuring out constructive ways of integrating our children, who all lived in different parts of the world. We decided to rent condominiums in a resort area and send them all plane tickets. Those who could come did; those who couldn't didn't. Eventually, the children all met each other and get along fine.

Not all of life was rosy. Two years after we got together, Phillip developed a nonmalignant tumor in his inner ear and needed neurosurgery. Needless to say, all of my old buttons were pushed—the feelings of fear, apprehension, and anxiety. But he came through the operation successfully and recuperated quickly.

Shortly before Phillip's surgery, Heidi, my new pet, developed a sarcoma, a cancer common to German shepherds, and was put to sleep. Heidi left my life as quickly as she had come into it. I was very sad.

A year or so after that, my mother became sick, and her health continued its downward spiral until she died. Phillip remained by my side as my mother's health failed. He spent a lot of time with my mother and gave her joy in the last years of her life. I will always be grateful to him for that. In addition, as my mother was close to death, my late husband's sister, the only living member of his family of origin, died of cancer.

Life transitions included some bright moments. At the same time that my mother was failing, my younger son was planning a wedding, which took place three weeks after my mother died, at a beautiful resort in the Napa Valley. It was an exquisite weekend, almost magical. Many of my late husband's friends even joined us in California to wish my son well as he married.

The nodal event for me was the rehearsal dinner, when my late husband's friends toasted my son, telling stories about his father and how much joy he would have been feeling if he had been there. These friends saw it as their privilege and duty to be present at these kinds of events to carry on my late husband's legacy. At the same event, my son very graciously and elegantly toasted my new mate, Phillip, and noted how grateful he was for Phillip's presence, which he said freed him to go on with his life, because he knew that someone was there to watch over me.

Shortly after the tragic events of September 11, 2001 (which followed the wedding by just ten days), I was presented with an opportunity to begin a therapy practice in New York. I took it and with Phillip's blessing and encouragement began a new aspect of my professional life.

My older son, who was working in New York at the time, patiently and kindly gave of himself, his time, and his expertise while I began to settle in. During my first year in New York I reconnected with old college friends and established new relationships, both personal and professional. My practice continues to grow and my research is expanding. I continue to learn from the people I meet.

I am away three days each week and Phillip continues to pursue his busy academic career. However, my life in my hometown is changing, as many of my friends are leaving the city and retiring to Florida. Phillip and I still live in my family home and experience the luxury of entertaining our adult children when they come home for holidays and visits.

That is my story. I was widowed more than a decade ago. I now have a new man in my life and a permanent relationship. We have integrated our families as best we could, given the children's life stages, places of residence, and busy careers. Our social circle includes some friends from my old life and many from my new life. Overall, the character of my life bears little resemblance to the way it was when my husband was alive.

Life is. I have few regrets. I am only sorry that my children did not have their father to mentor them through their adolescent years and to see them achieve during their college and early adult years. He would have had a great deal to be proud of.

I am very grateful and thankful to all the people who kindly gave of themselves, their time, and their knowledge to support and mentor me and my children through this major life change transition. We learned a lot about life in the process—we now understand that death, painful though it is, is an important part of life and that learning about death helps us appreciate and value life.

You now have the opportunity to craft your journey. You are free to follow your passions and your desires, to take your own risks. The options are endless. I wish you good fortune as you begin to craft the next chapter in your life.

References

Alan, G. 1944. Traditions and transitions. *Psychoanalytic Review* 81(1):79–100.

American Psychiatric Association. 1994. *Diagnostic and Psychiatric Manual of Mental Disorders (DSM-IV)*. 4ᵗʰ ed. Washington, D.C.: American Psychiatric Association.

Bowlby, J. 1969. *Attachment*. Vol. 1 of *Attachment and Loss*. New York: Basic Books.

———. 1973. *Separation, Anxiety, and Anger*. Vol. 2 of *Attachment and Loss*. London: Hogarth Press.

———. 1980. *Loss*. Vol. 3 of *Attachment and Loss*. New York: Basic Books.

Butz, M. 1992. The fractal nature of the development of the self. *Psychological Reports* 71(2/3):1043–63.

Campbell, J., P. Swank, and K. Vincent. 1991. Role of hardiness in resolution of grief. *Omega* 23:53–65.

Carstensen, L., and A. Freund. 1994. The resilience of the aging self. *Developmental Review* 14(1):81–92.

Dean, A., B. Kolodny, and P. Wood. 1991. Effects of social support from various sources on depression in elderly persons. *Social Work Abstracts* 27(2):870.

Elder, G. Jr. 1994. Time, human agency, and social change: Perspectives on the life course. *Social Psychology Quarterly* 57:4-15.

Furth, H. 1995. Self in which relation. *American Psychologist* 50(3):176.

Gallagher, D. E., J. A. Peterson, and L. W. Thompson. 1981–82. Psychological factors affecting adaptation to bereavement in the elderly. *International Journal of Aging & Human Development* 17(2):79–95.

George, L. 1993. Sociological perspectives in life transitions. *Annual Review of Sociology* 19:353-373.

Gilligan, C. 1982. *In a Different Voice: Psychological Theory and Women's Development.* Cambridge, Mass.: Harvard University Press.

Horowitz, M. 1990. Change in schemas in self and others. *Journal of the Psychoanalytic Association* 38(2):297–324.

Josselson, R. E. 1997. *Revising Herself.* New York: A. Knopf.

Kalish, R. A. 1982. Death and survivorship: The final transition. *Annals of the American Academy of Political and Social Science* 464:163–73.

Kohak, E. 1994. Life transitions. *Psychoanalytic Review* 81(1):101–24.

Kubler-Ross, E. 1997. *On Death and Dying.* New York: Scribner Classics.

Landau, R. 1991. The adjustment of younger widows who are also mothers. PhD diss., University of New Jersey.

Levinson, D. 1986. *Seasons of a Man's Life.* New York: Ballantine Books.

Levinson, D. 1997. Young widowhood: A life change journey. *Journal of Personal and Interpersonal Loss* 2:277–91.

———. 2002. *The Next Beginning.* Baltimore: Springbriar Institute.

Levinson, D., and H. G. Prigerson. 2000. Traumatic grief and the spousal loss model. *Journal of Illness, Crisis and Loss* 8(1):32–46.

Lieberman, M. 1998. *Doors Close, Doors Open: Widows, Grieving, and Growing.* New York: G. P. Putnam's Sons.

Lopata, H. 1996. *Current Widowhood: Myths and Realities.* Thousand Oaks, Calif.: Sage Publications.

———. 1973. *Widowhood in an American City.* Cambridge, Mass.: Schenkman Publishing Company.

Lowenstein, A., R. Landau, and A. Rosen. 1994. Adjustment to loss of a spouse as a multivariate construct. *Omega* 28(3):229–45.

Marwit, S., and D. Klass. 1995. Grief and the role of the inner representation of the deceased. *Omega* 30(4):283–98.

McGoldrick, M. 1989. *The Family Life Cycle.* Boston: Allyn and Bacon.

Morgan, L. S. 1980. Work in widowhood: A viable option? *The Gerontologist* 20(5):581–87.

Paul, N. L., and B. B. Paul. 1975. *A Marital Puzzle*. New York: W. W. Norton & Company, Inc.

Redfoot, D. L. 1987. On the separatin' place: Social class and relocation among older women. *Social Forces* 66(2):486–500.

Rosenberg, H. 1991. National Center for Health Statistics, Vital Statistics, Vol. II: Part A, Table 1–34.[ED: I'm not sure how to correctly format this reference. KS]

Rutter, M. 1987. Psychosocial resilience and protective mechanisms. *American Journal of Orthopsychiatry* 57(3):316–31.

Sable, P. 1991. Attachment, loss of spouse and elderly grief. *Omega* 23:129–40.

Sheehy, G. 1974. *Passages*. New York: E. P. Dutton & Company, Inc.

———. 1995. *New Passages: Mapping Your Life across Time*. New York: Ballantine Books.

Stroebe, W., M. Stroebe, G. Ahakounkin, and H. Schut. 1996. The role of loneliness and social support in adjustment of loss: A test of attachment versus stress theory. *Journal of Personality and Social Behavior* 70(6):19.

U.S. Census Bureau. 2000. Marital Status of People 15 Years and Over, by Age, Sex, Personal Earnings, Race and Hispanic Origin/1, March 2000.

Wan, T. T. H. 1984. Health consequences of major role losses in later life: A panel study. *Research on Aging* 6(4):469–89.

Watzlawik, P., J. Weakland, and R. Fisch. 1974. *Change*. New York: W. W. Norton & Co., Inc.

Wehr, T., A. Wirz-Justice, F. K. Goodwin, W. Duncan, and J. C. Gillin. 1979. Phase advance of the circadian sleep-wake cycle as an antidepressant. *Science* 206:710–13.

Zisook, S. 1987. *Adjustment to Widowhood: Biopsychosocial Aspects of Grief and Bereavement*. Washington, D.C.: American Psychiatric Press.

Some Other
New Harbinger Titles

The Power of Two Workbook, Item 3341 $19.95

Adult Children of Divorce, Item 3368 $14.95

Fifty Great Tips, Tricks, and Techniques to Connect with Your Teen, Item 3597 $10.95

Helping Your Child with OCD, Item 3325 $19.95

Helping Your Depressed Child, Item 3228 $14.95

The Couples's Guide to Love and Money, Item 3112 $18.95

50 Wonderful Ways to be a Single-Parent Family, Item 3082 $12.95

Caring for Your Grieving Child, Item 3066 $14.95

Helping Your Child Overcome an Eating Disorder, Item 3104 $16.95

Helping Your Angry Child, Item 3120 $17.95

The Stepparent's Survival Guide, Item 3058 $17.95

Drugs and Your Kid, Item 3015 $15.95

The Daughter-In-Law's Survival Guide, Item 2817 $12.95

Whose Life Is It Anyway?, Item 2892 $14.95

It Happened to Me, Item 2795 $17.95

Act it Out, Item 2906 $19.95

Parenting Your Older Adopted Child, Item 2841 $16.95

Boy Talk, Item 271X $14.95

Talking to Alzheimer's, Item 2701 $12.95

Helping a Child with Nonverbal Learning Disorder or Asperger's Syndrome, Item 2779 $14.95

The 50 Best Ways to Simplify Your Life, Item 2558 $11.95

When Anger Hurts Your Relationship, Item 2604 $13.95

The Couple's Survival Workbook, Item 254X $18.95

Loving Your Teenage Daughter, Item 2620 $14.95

Call **toll free, 1-800-748-6273,** or log on to our online bookstore at **www.newharbinger.com** to order. Have your Visa or Mastercard number ready. Or send a check for the titles you want to New Harbinger Publications, Inc., 5674 Shattuck Ave., Oakland, CA 94609. Include $4.50 for the first book and 75¢ for each additional book, to cover shipping and handling. (California residents please include appropriate sales tax.) Allow two to five weeks for delivery.

Prices subject to change without notice.